Better Homes and Gardens

CHRISTMAS
FROM THE HEART
Volume 24

Meredith Consumer Marketing
Des Moines, Iowa

CHRISTMAS
FROM THE HEART

MEREDITH CORPORATION CONSUMER MARKETING
Vice President, Consumer Marketing: Janet Donnelly
Consumer Marketing Product Director: Heather Sorensen
Consumer Marketing Product Manager: Tammy Hagerty
Consumer Marketing Billing/Renewal Manager: Tami Beachem
Business Director: Ron Clingman
Senior Production Manager: Al Rodruck
Photographers: Jay Wilde, Marty Baldwin, Jason Donnelly, Jacob Fox

WATERBURY PUBLICATIONS, INC.
Contributing Editor: Carol Field Dahlstrom
Contributing Food Stylists: Charles Worthington, Jennifer Peterson
Contributing Copy Editor: Terri Fredrickson
Contributing Proofreader: Peg Smith

Editorial Director: Lisa Kingsley
Creative Director: Ken Carlson
Associate Editors: Tricia Bergman, Mary Williams
Associate Design Director: Doug Samuelson
Production Assistant: Mindy Samuelson

BETTER HOMES AND GARDENS® MAGAZINE
Editor in Chief: Gayle Goodson Butler
Art Director: Michael D. Belknap
Senior Deputy Editor: Nancy Wall Hopkins
Editorial Assistant: Renee Irey

MEREDITH PUBLISHING GROUP
President: Tom Harty

MEREDITH CORPORATION
Chairman and Chief Executive Officer: Stephen M. Lacy

In Memoriam: E.T. Meredith III (1933–2003)

All of us at Meredith Consumer Marketing are dedicated to
providing you with information and ideas to enhance your home.
We welcome your comments and suggestions. Write to us at:
Meredith Consumer Marketing, 1716 Locust St., Des Moines, IA 50309-3023.

Contents

MAKING CHRISTMAS MEMORIES

Christmas is the happiest time of year as you gather with family and friends to share treasured holiday memories. We all remember the genuine pleasures of handmade gifts, warm flavors from the kitchen, twinkling lights, shiny ornaments, and majestic evergreen trees. We think back on the joyous Christmas cards we loved to read, the plate of cookies that a neighbor brought by on a snowy afternoon, and the quiet nights spent with friends and family filled with smiles and secrets.

Renew the spirit of Christmas in your home this year by making your holiday special with simply beautiful projects and recipes you make yourself. In this book you'll find ideas for crafting, decorating, cooking, and gift-giving. Try your hand at making a jingle bell and poinsettia wreath or stitch a rickrack Christmas stocking. String a sweet candy garland or create a candy cane centerpiece. Bake some bar cookies drizzled with chocolate and stir up some appetizers that are sure to please. Make this Christmas one that they will remember forever...a Christmas from the Heart.

The Editors

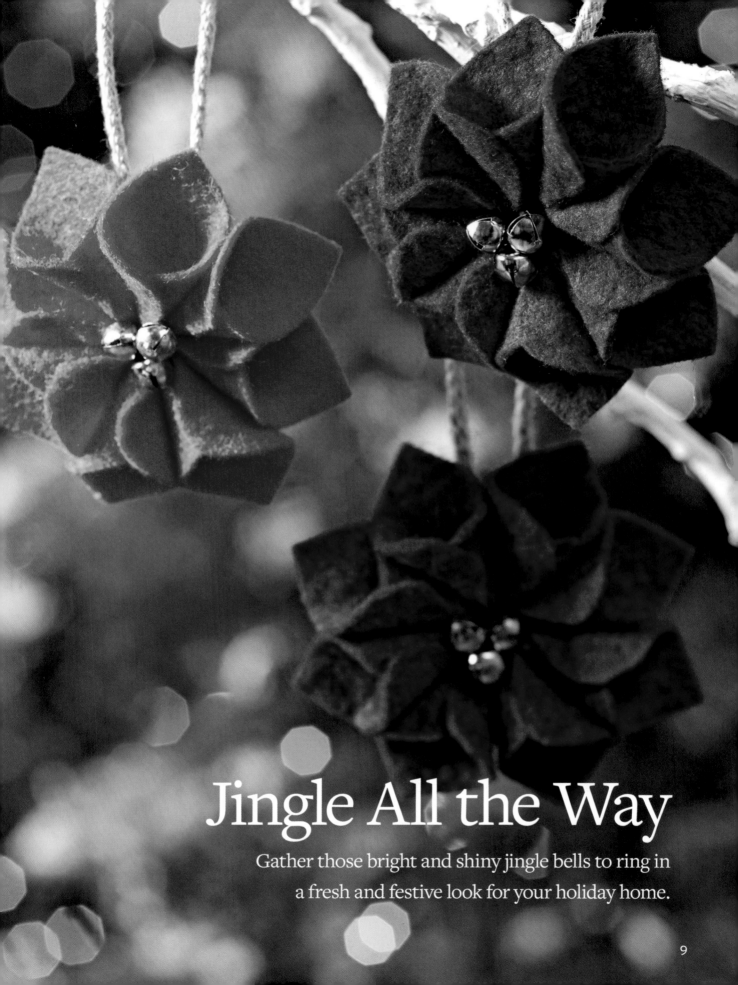

Jingle All the Way

Gather those bright and shiny jingle bells to ring in
a fresh and festive look for your holiday home.

Antiqued jingle bells in all sizes combine with soft, natural-color pom-poms to make a beautifully textured wreath to greet your holiday guests.

Jingling Pom-Pom Wreath

Create your own special color and texture on each jingle bell by layering paint and adding texture with a cotton ball.

WHAT YOU NEED

Large and medium-size gold and silver jingle bells • Box style wreath frame (wire wreath form) • Purchased pom-poms (or make your own) • Cotton balls • Black craft paint • Gold or bronze spray paint suitable for metal • Hot-glue gun and glue sticks • Yarn and needle large enough to accommodate yarn • 1½-inch-wide ribbon

WHAT YOU DO

1. To antique some of the jingle bells, paint them with gold or bronze spray paint. When dry, use a cotton ball to lightly dab the jingle bell with black paint. Wipe off immediately. Continue this process until jingle bell has desired level of antique look.

2. Attach antiqued and silver and gold bells to the wreath with a hot-glue gun. Hold each jingle bell in place until hot glue is dry to ensure a strong hold. When all jingle bells are in place, sew pom-poms onto the wreath form using yarn and needle.

3. Make a bow using the gold ribbon and hot-glue to the finished wreath.

Musical Picture Frame

Dozens of bells dress up a plain wood picture frame to add some jingle to your favorite holiday music.

WHAT YOU NEED
Purchased picture frame • Jingle bells in a variety of sizes, shapes, and colors • Hot-glue gun and glue sticks • Vintage Christmas sheet music • Pencil • Scissors • Crafts paint (optional)• Glitter (optional)

WHAT YOU DO
1. Remove glass from frame. Plan the arrangement of the bells on the frame. If desired, paint and glitter some of the bells. Let dry.
2. Using the hot-glue gun and glue sticks, adhere the bells at the corners of the frame, mixing the sizes of the bells as desired. Let dry.
3. Cut out the sheet music to fit inside the frame. Reassemble the picture frame.

Bowl of Bells

Let the color and sparkle of jingle bells reflect your holiday spirit. For a simple-to-make centerpiece, fill a shallow bowl with dozens of jingle bells and neutral color ornaments.

Flower Leaf Template
Cut 8

Flower Circle Template
Cut 1

Jingle Poinsettia Ornaments

Bits of soft red felt harmonize with shiny jingle bells to make stunning little poinsettias for your holiday tree.

WHAT YOU NEED (FOR ONE POINSETTIA)

⅛ yard of nonwoven felt such as National Nonwovens in desired shade of red • 3 mini jingle bells • Hot-glue gun and glue sticks • Medium weight rope-style twine

WHAT YOU DO

1. Copy and trace templates, above. Cut 8 flower leaf shapes and one flower circle from felt.

2. Wrap the left side of the leaf to the right (like a cone) and secure with a dot of hot glue. Repeat for all 8 pieces. Attach pieces, with the points at the center of the circle, around the circle using a hot-glue gun. Let dry.

3. Hot-glue 3 small jingle bells to the inside of the flower. To hang, attach a small piece of rope twine to the back of the flower with hot glue.

Jingle Poinsettia Wreath

Perfect little poinsettias encircle around to make a sweet little wreath for holiday decorating.

WHAT YOU NEED

7 Jingle Poinsettia Ornaments (see instructions, page 15) • 9-inch round flat wreath form • Hot-glue gun and glue sticks • 24 inches of ¾-inch wide ribbon • 8 inches of rope-style twine

WHAT YOU DO

1. Plan the arrangement of the flowers on the wreath form. Hot-glue the flowers in place.
2. Tie a bow with the ribbon and hot-glue in place. Hot-glue the rope-style twine to the back for hanging.

Bell-Trimmed Tweed Pillow

Inexpensive little jingle bells add the perfect touch to a red tweed pillow.

WHAT YOU NEED

Purchased or handmade pillow • Small gold jingle bells • Needle • Strong thread, such as monofilament thread

WHAT YOU DO

1. Purchase a small wool pillow or make your own. To make a 9-inch wool pillow, cut 2 pieces of fabric to measure 10×10 inches. With right sides together sew a ½-inch seam all around the edge, leaving a 3-inch opening for turning. Turn and press. Fill with poly fiberfill. Stitch opening closed.
2. Using a needle and strong thread, stitch the jingle bells along the seam line until all the edges are covered.

Jingle bells in gold and silver hues gently hang from printed gray and natural-color ribbons to signal that Christmas is near.

Ring the Bells Wall Decor

Bells ring holiday cheer as they dangle from festive ribbons inside a distressed picture frame.

WHAT YOU NEED

Large picture frame with no glass (this one is 18×24 inches) • Crafts paint in desired color (optional) • Patterned ribbon in desired widths and lengths • Jingle bells in desired sizes and colors • 2 small pieces of wood the width of the frame and about 4 inches long • Wood glue • Crafts glue • Clip clothespin • Double-stick tape

WHAT YOU DO

1. Prepare the picture frame as desired, painting and distressing the frame or leaving as purchased.
2. Glue the 2 small pieces of wood at the top and bottom of the frame. This will allow the bells to hang freely if hung close to a wall.
3. Lay the frame on a flat surface. Choose the jingle bells and arrange them inside the frame at random lengths. Cut the patterned ribbon to fit the chosen lengths. Slide the ribbon through the hole at the top of the bell and pull ribbon up about 2 inches. Glue ribbon together in place, securing with a clothespin until dry.
4. Use double-stick tape to secure the ribbons on the back side of the frame, adjusting as needed. Hang in a window or on a wall.

Jingle Bell Wreath

A twiggy birch wreath embellished with rusty jingle bells lends its free-flowing, casual form to a front door. A mix of ming pine and fir sprays studded with pinecones completes the look. A metallic bow layered atop a burlap bow adds textural interest.

WHAT YOU NEED

30-inch wispy birch wreath • Faux ming pine sprays with attached pinecones • Faux fir sprays • Hot-glue gun and glue sticks • Florist's wire • 2⅓ yards of 4-inch-wide wire-edge burlap ribbon • 1 yard metal ribbon • Rust-color jingle bells (one 3-inch and one 2-inch)

WHAT YOU DO

1. Insert the ming pine sprays into the wreath in a clockwise direction, allowing the wispy/twiggy ends to show. When satisfied with the look, hot-glue or wire the sprays to the wreath. Fill in with fir sprays, working clockwise. When satisfied with the look, hot-glue or wire the sprays to the wreath.

2. Wire or hot-glue a bow made from the burlap ribbon at the top of the wreath, placing it slightly off center. To make the bow, cut a 60-inch length of ribbon. Leaving an 8-inch tail, make a 7-inch loop, holding the ribbon between your thumb and index finger. Continue holding the ribbon, and make a second loop the same size in the opposite direction. Make another loop the same size in the same direction as the original loop. Wrap wire around the bow center, not trimming the wire ends. For the remaining bow tails, wire the remaining piece of ribbon to the center.

3. Center a bow made from the metal ribbon on top of the burlap bow. Make the loops 6 inches long and the tail 12 inches long. Wire the bow to the burlap bow.

4. Thread the bells onto a piece of florist's wire. Position the bells on top of the bows and wire in place. Trim the wire and ribbon ends.

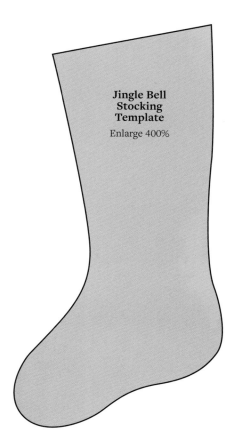

**Jingle Bell
Stocking
Template**
Enlarge 400%

Jingle Bell Stocking

You will hear Santa when he fills this stocking adorned in golden jingle bells.

WHAT YOU NEED

Tracing paper • Pencil • ½ yard of tweed wool fabric • ½ yard of black satin (for lining) • 20 small gold jingle bells • 2×24-inch piece of black twill fabric • Button thread • Needle • Narrow black ribbon • Scissors

WHAT YOU DO

1. Enlarge and trace template above, and cut out. Use the stocking template to cut a front and a back, reversing one of the shapes. Repeat for the lining. In addition, cut a 6×16-inch piece of tweed fabric for the cuff.
2. For the cuff ruffle, narrow hem one long edge of the black twill fabric. Gather the other long edge. Turn under one long edge of the cuff and baste in place. Lay the gathered edge of the black ruffle under the cuff and topstitch in place. Remove basting stitches. Turn back short edges of cuff and topstitch in place. Set cuff aside.
3. Stitch stocking pieces with right sides together, leaving top edge open, using a ½-inch seam. Clip curves. Turn right side out.
4. Stitch lining pieces with right sides together using ⅜-inch seam. Trim the seam close to stitching to reduce bulk in stocking. Insert lining inside turned stocking, keeping top straight edges even. Pin right side of cuff to inside lining of stocking and stitch. Turn cuff to outside of stocking and press.
5. Use button thread to sew jingle bells along bottom edge of cuff along black ruffle. Make a hanging loop using narrow black ribbon.

Jingle All the Way Table Setting

Jingle bells in a classic gold-and-white scheme bring a festive touch to your holiday table. Use bells as toppers for foam tree centerpieces which are coated with spray-on glue and glittery "snow." Napkins folded in triangular shapes and wrapped with ribbon continue the gold theme. A clear ornament filled with tiny bells and tagged with guests' initials doubles as a name card and a take-home favor.

Sweets by the Dozen

Making Christmas cookies brings out the inner baker in cooks of all persuasions. Whatever your passion, fill your cookie larder to overflowing with stunning treasures from this yummy selection.

Vanilla Bean Pretzels

Pearl sugar adds crunchy sweetness to these pretzel-shape cookies and looks just like the salt sprinkled on real pretzels.

WHAT YOU NEED

6	tablespoons butter, softened
½	cup granulated sugar
1	teaspoon baking powder
¼	teaspoon salt
3	egg yolks
2	teaspoons vanilla bean paste
½	cup milk
2½	cups all-purpose flour
1	egg, lightly beaten
1	tablespoon water
	Pearl decorating sugar or coarse decorating sugar

WHAT YOU DO

1. In a large mixing bowl beat butter with an electric mixer on medium to high for 30 seconds. Add granulated sugar, baking powder, and salt. Beat until combined, scraping sides of bowl occasionally. Beat in egg yolks and vanilla bean paste until combined. Gradually beat in milk until combined. Beat in as much of the flour as you can with the mixer. Using a wooden spoon, stir in any remaining flour (dough will be sticky). Divide dough in half. Cover and chill for at least 2 hours or until dough is easy to handle.
2. Preheat oven to 350°F. Lightly grease a cookie sheet; set aside. Working with one portion of dough at a time, pinch off 1-inch pieces of dough. On a lightly floured surface, roll each piece into a 9-inch rope. Make a U shape with the rope. Holding each rope end, cross one end over the other. Fold the ends to the bottom of the U shape. Moisten ends; press ends to bottom of the U to seal. Place pretzels 2 inches apart on the prepared cookie sheet.
3. In a small bowl combine egg and the water. Brush pretzels lightly with egg mixture; sprinkle with pearl sugar. Bake for 8 to 10 minutes or until firm and edges are lightly browned. Transfer to a wire rack; cool.
Makes 35 cookies.

French Pistachio Buttercreams

Rich buttercream filling sandwiched between crisp sugar cookies makes these treats just like those found in the finest Parisian patisseries.

WHAT YOU NEED

1½	cups all-purpose flour
¼	teaspoon salt
¾	cup butter, softened
½	cup powdered sugar
1	egg
	Granulated sugar
½	cup powdered sugar

¼	cup butter, softened
1	teaspoon brandy or milk
½	cup pistachio nuts, chopped

WHAT YOU DO

1. In a small bowl stir together flour and salt; set aside. In a medium mixing bowl beat the ¾ cup butter and ½ cup powdered sugar with an electric mixer on medium to high until combined. Beat in egg until combined. Beat in flour mixture on low just until combined. Cover; chill about 1 hour or until dough is easy to handle.
2. Preheat oven to 350°F. Shape dough into ¾- to 1-inch balls. Place balls on an ungreased cookie sheet. Dip the bottom of a glass in granulated sugar and flatten each ball to a 1½-inch circle. Bake for 7 to 10 minutes or until bottoms are lightly browned. Transfer cookies to a wire rack; cool.
3. Meanwhile, for filling, in a small mixing bowl beat ½ cup powdered sugar, the ¼ cup butter, and the brandy with an electric mixer on medium to high until smooth.
4. Spread filling on bottoms of half of the cookies. Top with the remaining cookies, bottom sides down. Roll edges of sandwich cookies in pistachios. Chill about 30 minutes more or until filling is set. **Makes 20 sandwich cookies.**

Chocolate-Marshmallow Cookies

Marshmallow filling oozes from these chocolate-iced drops.

WHAT YOU NEED
½   cup butter, softened
½   cup shortening
1   cup granulated sugar
½   cup packed brown sugar
1   teaspoon baking soda
½   teaspoon salt
2   eggs
1   teaspoon vanilla
¼   cup unsweetened cocoa powder
2½   cups all-purpose flour
½   of a 7-ounce jar marshmallow creme
1½   cups semisweet chocolate pieces
¾   cup sweetened condensed milk
1   tablespoon milk
     Milk (optional)

WHAT YOU DO
1. Preheat oven to 375°F. In a large mixing bowl beat butter and shortening with an electric mixer on medium to high for 30 seconds. Add granulated sugar, brown sugar, baking soda, and salt. Beat until combined, scraping sides of bowl occasionally. Beat in eggs and vanilla until combined. Beat in cocoa powder. Beat in as much of the flour as you can with the mixer. Using a wooden spoon, stir in any remaining flour.

2. Drop dough by rounded teaspoons 2 inches apart onto an ungreased cookie sheet. Spoon marshmallow creme into a pastry bag fitted with a small round (¼-inch) tip. Insert tip into each dough mound and squeeze marshmallow creme into dough.

3. Bake for 8 to 9 minutes or until edges are firm. Cool for 2 minutes. Transfer cookies to a wire rack; cool.

4. For icing, in a small saucepan cook and stir chocolate pieces and sweetened condensed milk over low heat until melted and smooth. Stir in the 1 tablespoon milk. If necessary, stir in additional milk, ½ teaspoon at a time, to reach glazing consistency. Spread cookies with icing. Let stand until icing is set. **Makes 48 cookies.**

Pumpkin-Pecan Cookies

A swirl of sweet brown sugar frosting tops these soft spiced pumpkin cookies. If you like, substitute walnuts for the pecans.

WHAT YOU NEED
2   cups all-purpose flour
1½   teaspoons baking powder
1   teaspoon ground cinnamon
¼   teaspoon baking soda
¼   teaspoon ground allspice
1   cup butter, softened
1   cup granulated sugar
1   egg
1   cup canned pumpkin
1   cup chopped pecans, toasted*
1   recipe Brown-Sugar Butter Frosting

WHAT YOU DO
1. Preheat oven to 375°F. In a bowl stir together flour, baking powder, cinnamon, soda, and allspice; set aside.

2. In a large mixing bowl beat butter with an electric mixer on medium to high for 30 seconds. Add sugar. Beat until combined, scraping sides of bowl occasionally. Beat in egg and pumpkin until combined. Using a wooden spoon, stir in flour mixture and pecans.

3. Drop dough by rounded teaspoons 2 inches apart onto an ungreased cookie sheet. Bake about 10 minutes or until bottoms are lightly browned. Cool on cookie sheet for 2 minutes. Transfer to a wire rack; cool. Spread cookies with Brown Sugar-Butter Frosting. **Makes 55 cookies.**

Brown Sugar-Butter Frosting In a medium saucepan cook and stir 6 tablespoons butter and ⅓ cup packed brown sugar over medium heat until butter is melted and mixture is smooth. Remove from heat. Stir in 2 cups powdered sugar and 1 teaspoon vanilla. Stir in enough hot water (3 to 4 teaspoons) to reach spreading consistency. Immediately spread frosting over cooled cookies. If frosting becomes grainy, add a few more drops of hot water and stir frosting until smooth.

***Tip:** To toast nuts, spread them in a shallow baking pan. Bake in a 350°F oven for 5 to 10 minutes or until light brown, shaking pan once or twice. Watch carefully so the nuts don't burn.

Caramel- and Coconut-Topped Cookies

Melted caramels and toasted coconut give these tender, buttery cookies a candylike topping. Store them in a tightly covered container layered with waxed paper to prevent sticking.

WHAT YOU NEED
½   cup shortening
½   cup butter, softened
½   cup granulated sugar
½   cup packed brown sugar
1   teaspoon baking powder
¼   teaspoon salt
⅛   teaspoon baking soda
1   egg
2   tablespoons milk
1   teaspoon vanilla
1¾ cups all-purpose flour
36 vanilla caramels, unwrapped
¼   cup milk
¼   cup shredded coconut, toasted*

WHAT YOU DO
1. Preheat oven to 350°F. Line a cookie sheet with parchment paper; set aside.
2. In a large mixing bowl beat shortening and butter with an electric mixer on medium to high for 30 seconds. Add granulated sugar, brown sugar, baking powder, salt, and baking soda. Beat until combined, scraping sides of bowl occasionally. Beat in egg, the 2 tablespoons milk, and the vanilla until combined. Beat in as much of the flour as you can with the mixer. Using a wooden spoon, stir in any remaining flour.
3. Drop dough by level measuring tablespoons 2 inches apart onto the prepared cookie sheet. Bake for 9 minutes. Transfer to a wire rack.
4. Meanwhile, in a small heavy saucepan cook and stir caramels and the ¼ cup milk over medium-low heat until smooth. Spoon 1 teaspoon of the caramel mixture onto each cookie; tilt cookie so caramel flows to within ¼ inch of the edges. Sprinkle with coconut; cool.
Makes 40 cookies.
*Tip: To toast coconut, spread the coconut in a shallow baking pan. Bake in a 350°F oven for 5 to 10 minutes or until lightly browned, shaking pan once or twice. Watch carefully so the coconut doesn't burn.

Orange Cookie Batons

These melt-in-your-mouth buttery sticks lend variety to a plate of round cookies. You'll need a cookie press to shape them.

WHAT YOU NEED
1½ cups butter, softened
1   cup granulated sugar
1   teaspoon baking powder
1   egg

2   teaspoons finely shredded orange peel
1   teaspoon vanilla
3½ cups all-purpose flour
    Powdered sugar

WHAT YOU DO
1. Preheat oven to 375°F. In a large mixing bowl beat butter with an electric mixer on medium to high for 30 seconds. Add granulated sugar and baking powder. Beat until combined, scraping sides of bowl occasionally. Beat in egg, orange peel, and vanilla. Beat in as much of the flour as you can with the mixer. Using a wooden spoon, stir in any remaining flour.
2. Pack unchilled dough into a cookie press fitted with a small star plate (the plate should contain one cutout star, not multiple cutouts that form a star design). Force dough through press onto an ungreased cookie sheet, cutting 5- to 6-inch-long sticks and spacing sticks ½ inch apart.
3. Bake for 8 to 10 minutes or until edges are firm but not brown. Transfer cookies to a wire rack; cool. Sprinkle cookies with powdered sugar before serving.
Makes 40 cookies.

Stir in vanilla and orange peel. Stir in flour and pecans. Spread batter evenly in prepared baking pan.

3. Bake for 28 to 30 minutes or until top is lightly browned and edges start to pull away from sides of pan. Cool in pan on a wire rack. Spread Citrusy White Chocolate Frosting over cooled brownies. Using the edges of the foil, lift uncut brownies out of pan. Cut into bars. If desired, garnish with kumquat slices before serving. **Makes 32 brownies.**

Citrusy White Chocolate Frosting In a small saucepan cook and stir 6 ounces chopped white chocolate with cocoa butter over low heat until melted and smooth. Remove from heat; cool. Meanwhile, in a large mixing bowl beat 2 cups powdered sugar and ½ cup softened butter with an electric mixer on low until smooth. Beat in ⅓ cup sour cream, ½ teaspoon orange flavoring, and ¼ teaspoon salt. Beat in 1½ cups additional powdered sugar until combined. Beat in the melted white chocolate.

Peppermint Marshmallow Brownies

If you can't find peppermint-flavor marshmallows, use plain ones. You will have a white topping and a little less peppermint flavor but the brownies will be equally tasty.

WHAT YOU NEED

3	ounces unsweetened chocolate, coarsely chopped
½	cup butter
1	cup sugar
2	eggs
¼	teaspoon peppermint extract
⅔	cup all-purpose flour
¼	teaspoon baking soda
1	cup peppermint-flavor tiny marshmallows
	Semisweet chocolate, melted (optional)

WHAT YOU DO

1. In a medium saucepan cook and stir unsweetened chocolate and butter over low heat until melted and smooth. Remove from heat; cool. Preheat oven to 350°F. Line an 8×8×2-inch baking pan with foil, extending the foil over edges of pan. Grease foil; set pan aside.

2. Preheat oven to 350°F. Line an 8×8×2-inch baking pan with foil, extending foil over edges of pan. Grease foil; set aside.

3. Stir sugar into cooled chocolate mixture. Add eggs, one at a time, beating with a wooden spoon after each addition just until combined. Stir in peppermint extract. In a small bowl stir together flour and baking soda; stir flour mixture into chocolate mixture just until combined. Pour batter into the prepared baking pan, spreading evenly.

4. Bake for 25 minutes. Immediately sprinkle with marshmallows. Bake for 3 to 4 minutes more or just until marshmallows are softened. Cool in pan on a wire rack.

5. Using the edges of the foil, lift uncut brownies out of pan. If desired, drizzle melted semisweet chocolate over cooled brownies. Let stand until chocolate is set. Cut into bars. **Makes 24 brownies.**

Citrusy White Chocolate Brownies

Instead of kumquats, top these brownies with small pieces of thinly sliced oranges or shredded orange peel.

WHAT YOU NEED

12	ounces white baking chocolate with cocoa butter, chopped
½	cup butter
½	cup sugar
3	eggs
2	teaspoons vanilla
2	teaspoons finely shredded orange peel
1½	cups all-purpose flour
½	cup finely chopped pecans, toasted (See Tip, page 28)
1	recipe Citrusy White Chocolate Frosting
	Thinly sliced kumquats (optional)

WHAT YOU DO

1. In a medium saucepan cook and stir white chocolate and butter over low heat until melted and smooth. Remove from heat; cool. Preheat oven to 350°F. Line a 13×9×2-inch baking pan with foil, extending the foil over edges of pan; set aside.

2. Stir sugar into white chocolate mixture. Add eggs, one at a time, beating with a wooden spoon after each addition.

Lemon Curd Crunch Bars

The addition of lemon curd and lemon peel offers a tangy punch to these much loved cereal bars.

WHAT YOU NEED

¼   cup butter
1   10-ounce package tiny marshmallows
¾   cup lemon curd
2   teaspoons finely shredded lemon peel
7   cups crisp rice cereal
¾   cup powdered sugar
3   to 4 teaspoons milk
     Crushed lemon drops (optional)

WHAT YOU DO

1. Line a 13×9×2-inch baking pan with foil, extending the foil over edges of pan. Lightly butter foil; set pan aside.
2. In a 4-quart heavy Dutch oven melt the ¼ cup butter over low heat. Stir in marshmallows. Cook and stir until marshmallows are melted. Stir in lemon curd and 1 teaspoon of the lemon peel until combined. Add cereal, stirring gently to coat.
3. Transfer cereal mixture to the prepared baking pan. Using a buttered spatula or buttered piece of waxed paper, press mixture very firmly and evenly into pan.
4. For icing, in a small bowl stir together powdered sugar and the remaining 1 teaspoon lemon peel. Stir in enough of the milk for icing to reach drizzling consistency. Drizzle over bars in pan. If desired, sprinkle with crushed lemon drops; press down gently. Let stand until icing is set.
5. Using the edges of the foil, lift uncut bars out of pan. Using a long buttered knife, cut into bars. **Makes 32 bars.**

Almond Spirals

These red and white spirals take a little more time than most slice-and-bake cookies but are worth the effort. You can store the unbaked dough rolls for up to 3 months. Thaw in the refrigerator before baking.

WHAT YOU NEED

¾   cup butter, softened
1   cup sugar
½   teaspoon baking powder
¼   teaspoon salt
1   egg
1   teaspoon vanilla
½   teaspoon almond extract
2   cups all-purpose flour
     Red paste food coloring
¼   cup ground almonds

WHAT YOU DO

1. In a large mixing bowl beat butter with an electric mixer on medium to high for 30 seconds. Add sugar, baking powder, and salt. Beat until combined, scraping bowl occasionally. Beat in egg, vanilla, and almond extract until combined. Beat in as much of the flour as you can with the mixer. Using a wooden spoon, stir in any remaining flour.
2. Divide dough in half. Tint one portion of dough using red food coloring. Stir or knead ground almonds into the remaining dough portion. Cover each portion and chill about 1 hour or until dough is easy to handle. Divide each portion in half.
3. Between two sheets of waxed paper, roll one portion of the red dough into a 12×8-inch rectangle. Repeat using one portion of almond dough. Remove the top sheets of waxed paper. Invert one rectangle on top of the other; press together gently to seal. Remove the remaining sheet of waxed paper. Tightly roll up rectangle, starting from a long side; pinch seam to seal. Repeat with the remaining portions of dough. Wrap each roll in waxed paper or plastic wrap. Chill about 3 hours or until dough is firm enough to slice.
4. Preheat oven to 375°F. Grease a cookie sheet. Cut rolls into ¼-inch slices. Place slices 2 inches apart on the prepared cookie sheet. Bake about 8 minutes or until tops are set. Cool on cookie sheet for 1 minute. Transfer cookies to a wire rack; cool. **Makes 70 cookies.**

Devilish Delights

These melt-in-your mouth treasures get a triple blast of flavor from two types of chocolate and a splash of coffee liqueur. Shown on page 25.

WHAT YOU NEED
6   tablespoons all-purpose flour
½   teaspoon baking powder
⅛   teaspoon salt
2   eggs
½   cup granulated sugar
1   to 2 tablespoons coffee liqueur or strong brewed espresso
2   teaspoons vanilla
10   ounces bittersweet chocolate, chopped
2   tablespoons butter
1   teaspoon instant espresso coffee powder
12   ounces dark chocolate, chopped
      Powdered sugar (optional)

WHAT YOU DO
1. Preheat oven to 350°F. Lightly grease a cookie sheet or line a cookie sheet with parchment paper; set aside. In a small bowl stir together flour, baking powder, and salt; set aside. In a large mixing bowl beat eggs, granulated sugar, coffee liqueur, and vanilla with an electric mixer on medium until combined. Set aside.
2. In a medium heavy saucepan cook and stir bittersweet chocolate, butter, and espresso coffee powder over medium-low heat until melted and smooth. Remove from heat. Whisk melted chocolate mixture into egg mixture until combined. Stir in flour mixture just until combined. Stir in dark chocolate (dough will resemble a thick brownie batter).
3. Drop dough by heaping teaspoons 2 inches apart onto the prepared cookie sheet. Bake for 8 to 9 minutes or until tops appear dry and centers remain soft. Cool on cookie sheet for 3 minutes. Transfer cookies to a wire rack; cool. If desired, sprinkle cookies lightly with powdered sugar.
Makes 36 cookies.
To Store: Do not sprinkle cookies with powdered sugar. Layer plain cookies between sheets of waxed paper in an airtight container; cover. Store at room temperature for up to 3 days or freeze for up to 3 months. To serve, thaw cookies, if frozen. If desired, sprinkle cookies with powdered sugar.

Hazelnut Sacher Brownies

A hazelnut crust and fudgy brownie layer stand in for the traditional cake in this twist on classic Sacher torte. The result is so rich that bite-size squares are the perfect serving size.

WHAT YOU NEED
¾   cup powdered sugar
½   cup butter, softened
¾   cup all-purpose flour
½   cup hazelnuts, toasted* and finely ground
¾   cup apricot preserves
3   ounces unsweetened chocolate, coarsely chopped
½   cup butter
1   egg
1   egg yolk
1   cup granulated sugar
¼   teaspoon salt
1   teaspoon vanilla
½   cup all-purpose flour
6   ounces semisweet chocolate, melted
1   ounce white baking chocolate with cocoa butter, melted

WHAT YOU DO
1. Preheat oven to 350°F. Line a 13×9×2-inch baking pan with foil, extending the foil over edges of pan. Grease foil; set pan aside.
2. For crust, in a small mixing bowl beat powdered sugar and the ½ cup softened butter with an electric mixer on low to medium until smooth. Beat in the ¾ cup flour and the ground nuts until combined. Press mixture onto the bottom of the prepared baking pan. Bake for 12 minutes. Cool in pan on a wire rack.
3. Place preserves in a blender or food processor. Cover and blend or process until smooth. Spread pureed preserves over crust. Chill for 20 minutes.
4. Meanwhile, in a small saucepan cook and stir the unsweetened chocolate and the ½ cup butter over low heat until melted and smooth. Remove from heat; cool for 10 minutes. In a medium mixing bowl beat egg, egg yolk, granulated sugar, and salt on medium for 5 minutes. Beat in the melted unsweetened chocolate and vanilla. Stir in the ½ cup flour just until combined. Carefully spread mixture over chilled preserves. Bake for 20 minutes more. Cool in pan on a wire rack.
5. Using the edges of the foil, lift uncut brownies out of pan. Spread brownies with melted semisweet chocolate; let stand until chocolate is set. Drizzle with melted white chocolate; let stand until white chocolate is set. Cut into bars. **Makes 48 brownies.**
*Tip: To toast hazelnuts, preheat oven to 350°F. Spread nuts in a single layer in a shallow baking pan. Bake for 8 to 10 minutes or until lightly toasted, stirring once to toast evenly. Cool slightly. Place warm nuts on a clean kitchen towel; rub with the towel to remove the loose skins.

Beautiful Birds & Berries

Lovely motifs of holiday birds and colorful berries mingle to create a festive home that reflects the beauty of nature.

Printed Paper Bird Trims

Printed vintage papers become elegant designs on 3-D birds for your holiday tree.

WHAT YOU NEED

Medium-weight printed paper (scrapbook paper or copies made from copyright-free vintage papers printed on both sides) • Pencil • Scissors • Waxed paper, crafts glue, fine glitter (optional) • Small paper punch • 10 inches of narrow ribbon in desired color

WHAT YOU DO

1. Choose scrapbook paper with all-over designs. Or copy vintage paper designs that you like. Enlarge and trace the templates right, and copy onto the printed paper. Cut out. Cut a slit on the bird wing and on the bird as marked on the templates.

2. If desired, lay the pieces on waxed paper and run a thin line of glue around the edge of each piece; dust with glitter. Let dry.

3. Slide the wings onto the body of the bird. Punch a hole in the top of the bird and thread the ribbon through the hole for hanging.

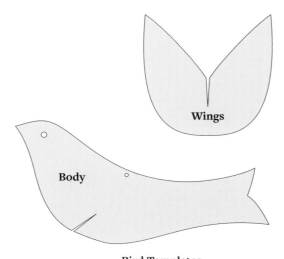

Wings

Body

Bird Templates
Enlarge all templates
200%

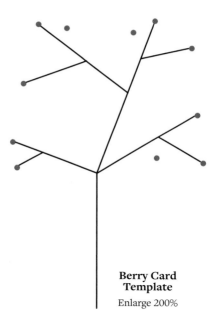

**Berry Card
Template**
Enlarge 200%

Sequin Berry Card

Tiny sequins, clustered like berries, make a sweet little berry tree greeting card.

WHAT YOU NEED

Pencil • Embroidery floss in red and brown • Red sequins • Blank card in brown or light brown • Needle • Scissors • Label maker with red label tape

WHAT YOU DO

1. Using the template, above left, as a guide, lightly sketch the tree onto the front of the card.
2. Use brown embroidery floss to stitch a long running stitch line over the pencil lines, knotting in the back. Where indicated, use red embroidery floss to sew red sequins using a French knot. Trim any threads on back of card.
3. Make a red label with desired greeting using label maker. Attach to front of card.

"For the Birds" Gift Jar

Bird lovers will love this gift of birdseed in a pretty little jar to share with their feathered friends.

WHAT YOU NEED
Glass jar • Small sheet of paper • Scissors • Pencil • Adhesive paper such as Contact paper • Black spray paint, suitable for glass • Birdseed • Bakers' twine • Tag

WHAT YOU DO
1. Copy the templates, right, to desired size to fit the side of the glass jar. Cut a large square of contact paper big enough to cover the side of the jar. Trace the oval template on that square and cut out the oval shape, leaving the square of adhesive paper. Carefully adhere that square with the open oval to the side of the jar.
2. Trace and cut the bird silhouette template out of adhesive paper. Affix the bird shape to glass jar inside the oval. Spray paint over the adhesive paper with black spray paint. Let dry. Remove contact paper;
3. Fill the jar with birdseed and tie the tag with bakers' twine to the jar lid.

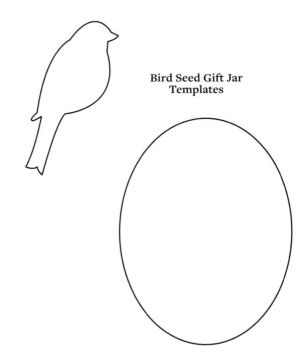

Bird Seed Gift Jar Templates

Appliqué Birds and Berries Table Runner

Birds and berries in soft teal and berry red combine to make an heirloom-quality piece for your holiday table.

WHAT YOU NEED

Final size is 20×14-inch oval
21×15-inch winter white wool for background • 5-inch square medium teal wool for birds • 4-inch square light teal wool for wings and tails • 4-inch square each 2 dusty green wools for leaves • 8×2-inch medium brown wool for stems and beak • 4-inch square red wool for berries • ½ yard white or off-white cotton for interfacing and backing • 3 yards paper-backed fusible web • Light teal, dark teal, golden brown, and yellow, size 12 or 30 cotton thread

WHAT YOU DO

Preparing Background

1. Following the directions on the template on page 46, trace oval on paper side of paper-backed fusible web. Cut out ¼ inch beyond traced line.
2. Cut the backing fabric into two 21×18-inch rectangles. Following manufacturer's directions, fuse background template to one rectangle. Cut out on traced line. Remove paper backing.
3. Carefully fuse to white wool. Press both sides to ensure fusing. Cut out on the edge of the cotton.

Preparing Appliqué

1. Using the appliqué templates on page 46 and tracing like pieces in groups on paper side of fusible web, trace 2 birds, 2 wings, 2 tails, 2 beaks, 8 large leaves, 6 small leaves, and 32 berries.
2. Cut excess fusible web from around groups. Fuse according to manufacturer's directions (except for the beaks) to the corresponding wool listed in materials. Cut out each piece on the traced line.
3. Cut a 7×1½-inch strip of paper-backed fusible web. Fuse according to manufacturer's directions to the brown wool along with the 2 beaks. Cut out beaks on the traced line. Positioning lengthwise on the fused paper, cut four 7×¼-inch strips.

Arranging and Stitching Appliqué

1. Remove the paper backing just before you arrange the appliqué.
2. Refer to the layout on page 47 to arrange all appliqué pieces and the photos on pages 44 and 45 for the stitching.
3. Fuse stems on the prepared background curving as indicated and butting 2 pieces of stem strip to make length of stem. Straight stitch down the center of the stems with brown thread.
4. With the brown thread and a triple stitch, stitch the dashed twig lines.
5. Arrange leaves on the stems placing one of the larger leaves over the stem joint. For the leaves, straight stitch over the stem stitching, stitching veins as shown as you come to each leaf, and continue up the stem to the top leaf.
6. With the brown thread stitch a line on each beak.
7. Using a blanket stitch with a wider (4.5) and longer (4) stitch than the programmed stitch, stitch around each bird body with light teal thread.
8. Blanket stitch around each wing with medium teal thread. Straight stitch about ⅛ inch from the edges of each tail and up the center.
9. With the medium teal thread triple stitch the bird legs.
10. Position the berries and straight stitch a cross through the centers with yellow thread.

Finishing

1. Place a large piece of fusible web over the back and fuse to the oval. Cut around the oval. Remove paper.
2. Fuse the backing cotton to the oval. Carefully cut the backing fabric to the edge of the oval making a very smooth edge.
3. Using the light teal thread on top and in the bobbin and the larger blanket stitch, stitch around the edge.

TIPS FOR A PERFECT APPLIQUÉ

• With the white background be sure your ironing board is clean. Place a piece of muslin or light fabric over board.

• After stitching, pull threads to back, knot and trim.

• For machine appliqué with this heavy thread use a 30 or 50 weight thread in the bobbin. Adjust the top tension as necessary. Make a stitch sample of the threads, stitches, and tension setting.

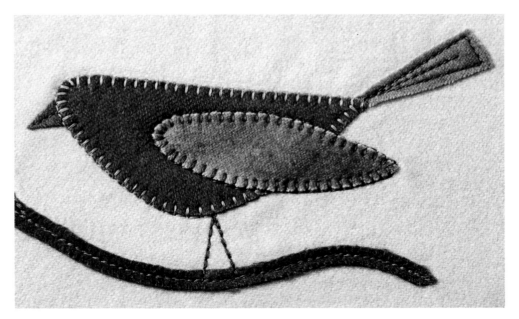

Stylized birds and berries in subtle colors of wool are appliquéd onto winter white wool and then hand-stitched for an elegant look.

Bird Templates
templates are reversed

Beak

Wing

Body

Tail

Berry

Large Leaf

Small Leaf

Fold

Bird and Berries Oval Template
Enlarge 300%

To make a complete oval fold a 22×17 inch piece of paper-backed fusible web in half in both directions. Place the folded edges on these dashed fold lines. Trace on the solid line. Cut out ¼ inch beyond traced line.

Fold

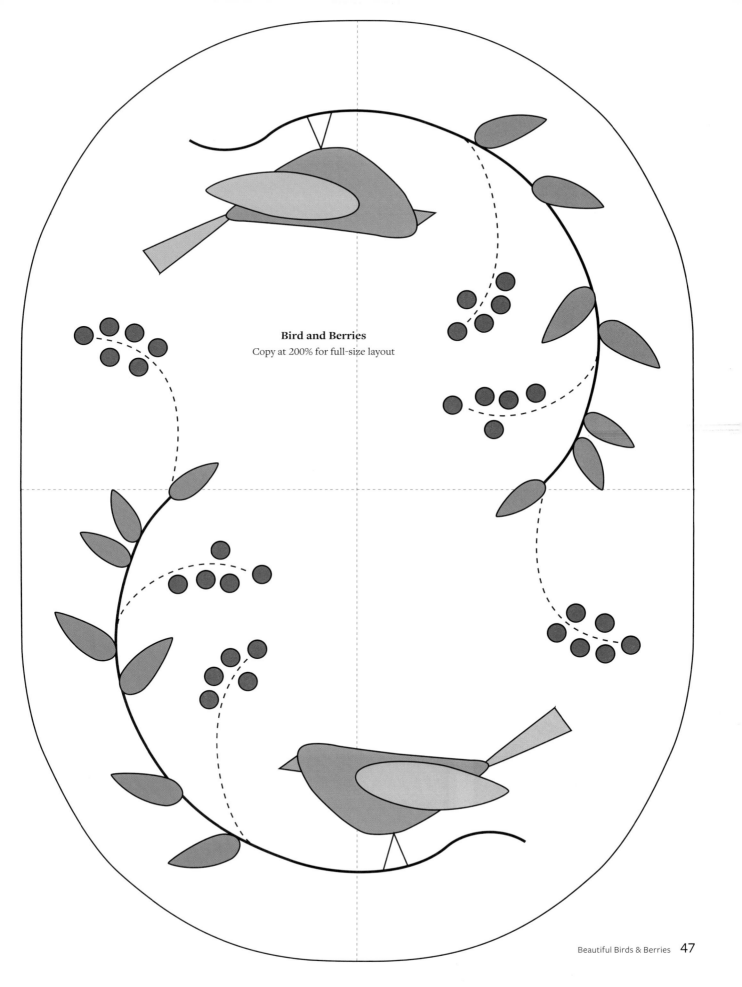

Bird and Berries

Copy at 200% for full-size layout

Little red pompoms look like colorful berries when they are scattered across natural branches with a dusting of copper color glitter.

Pom-Pom Berry Branches

Choose a bottle in the shape you like and spray with metallic paint to hold the sparkling berried branches.

WHAT YOU NEED
Natural branches, found outdoors or purchased at garden stores • Bottle • Copper-color spray paint • Decoupage medium such as Mod Podge • Foam brush • Copper-color glitter • Mini red pom-poms • Hot-glue gun and glue sticks • Red-and-white bakers' twine

WHAT YOU DO
1. Choose branches long enough to fit in the chosen bottle. Set branches aside.
2. Spray paint bottle with copper-color spray paint. Let dry.
3. Using a foam brush, coat branches with a light coat of decoupage medium and dust with copper-color glitter. Let dry.
4. Use a hot-glue gun to attach mini pom-poms onto the branches at random intervals. Let dry. Place in painted bottle. Tie bakers' twine around the neck of the bottle.

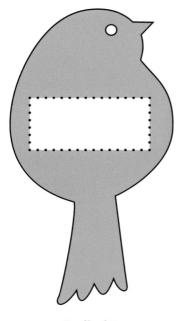

Cardinal Tag

Clever Cardinal Wraps

The lovely red cardinal and winter berries inspired these three pretty looks.

WHAT YOU NEED
Wide red ribbon • Silk flowers with berries • Red cardstock • White cardstock • Narrow ribbon • Velvet ribbon • Hot-glue gun and glue sticks • Red-and-white bakers' twine • Small picture frame

WHAT YOU DO
1. *For bow package,* make 2, two-loop bows from the wide red ribbon, one slightly larger than the other. Hot-glue them together and embellish with silk flowers.

2. *For the cardinal package,* copy the cardinal tag, upper right, and cut out of red cardstock. Add a white rectangle in the center and add the recipient's name. Adorn the cardinal tag with a narrow ribbon tied into a bow around the bird's neck. Tape to the package atop a velvet ribbon.

3. *For the cardinal in a frame,* copy the cardinal card, right. Write the recipient's name on the card. Place in a flat-back frame and tape or hot-glue it to the package.

Cardinal Card

Clay birds don a texture of lace and soft pastel colors to be used as ornaments or tucked into a pretty white Christmas berry wreath.

Golden Ceramic Bird Trims

Lightweight stone clay works perfectly for these air-dried clay birds that make beautiful little holiday trims.

WHAT YOU NEED
Lightweight stone clay • Fabric doily • Waxed paper • Crafts knife such as Xacto knife • Wooden skewer • Rolling pin • 220-grit sandpaper • Watercolor paints • Gold craft paint • Paper towels • Narrow ribbon • Tiny colorful buttons • Crafts glue

WHAT YOU DO
1. Copy bird template, right, and cut out. Set aside.
2. With a rolling pin, roll lightweight stone clay out to approximately ¼ inch thick. Place fabric doily onto the clay and continue to lightly roll until template has been embossed into clay.
3. Gently lay the bird template onto the clay and cut around the bird with a crafts knife. Use a skewer to poke a hole for the ribbon if using as an ornament. (If using in wreath, do not add hole.) Transfer to a surface covered with waxed paper to dry per package instructions.
4. When dry, sand any rough edges. Paint with watercolors as desired. When watercolor paint is dry, use gold paint to paint the doily-stamped area. Quickly wipe off with a paper towel to create the rustic effect.
5. Glue button on bird head for eye. Let dry. Thread ribbon through hole for hanging or place on wreath.

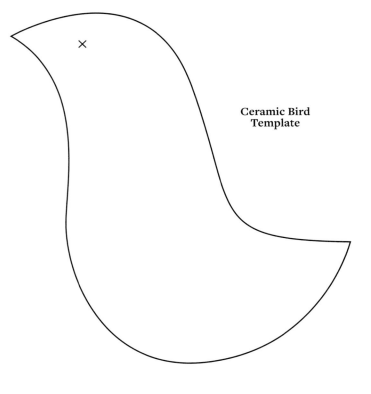

Ceramic Bird Template

MERRY CHRISTMAS

JOY

TRIM THE TREE

Fresh Shades of Green

Be a design trendsetter and make shifting shades of green your
holiday color scheme this Christmas season.

Lacy Plant Trio

Little bits of lace and shades of green spray paint turn ordinary jars into festive little containers.

WHAT YOU NEED

Small glass jars • Shades of green spray paint, suitable for glass • Gold spray paint, suitable for glass • Scraps of lace with open areas • Spray adhesive • Small evergreen • Dirt

WHAT YOU DO

1. Be sure the jars are clean and dry. Spray paint the outside of each jar with desired shade of green spray paint. Let dry.

2. Wrap lace around each jar and adhere with a light coat of spray adhesive. Spray paint through the lace with gold spray paint and let dry. Remove the lace.

3. Position a small evergreen sprig in the center of each jar and place dirt around the sprig, packing the dirt around it to secure the sprig. Add a little water. Note: Even though the sprig of evergreen has no roots, the water will keep the evergreen fresher through the season.

Add texture and subtle changes of green hues to simple jars by laying scraps of lace on the surface and painting over the lace. Then add sprigs of evergreen for a fresh holiday centerpiece.

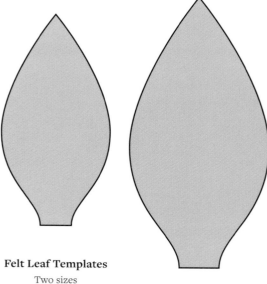

Felt Leaf Templates
Two sizes

Fresh-Picked Felt Wreath

Soft felt in green tones from cool mint green to warm leafy green combine to make a stunning holiday wreath.

WHAT YOU NEED
12-inch round-edge foam (or desired size) wreath form such as Styrofoam • Shades of green nonwoven felt such as National Nonwovens • Small jingle bells • Spray paint in green and teal • Hot-glue gun and glue sticks • Scissors • 1½×18-inch strip of felt in desired color for bow • Small ornaments, ribbon, jingle bells for hanging inside of wreath (optional)

WHAT YOU DO
1. Copy and use the desired template, above left, as a guide to cut out leaf shapes from green felt. Use the size that best fits the wreath form you have chosen. Cut approximately 300 leaf shapes from desired colors of green-tone felt.
2. Using the hot-glue gun to secure, attach one row of leaves around the wreath form mixing the colors of felt or changing the colors from light to dark. Continue this process until the wreath is covered.
3. Paint the bells a shade of green or teal. Let dry. Use hot glue to adhere them to the felt, grouping the bells in clusters.
4. Tie a bow with the strip of felt. Group bells and small ornaments on a narrow ribbon and hot-glue to top of wreath, if desired. Glue felt bow to top of wreath.

Mossy Elegance

This mossy green table setting has a fairy-tale quality, with tinges of gold lending sparkle to the gradations of green color. A tiny thyme wreath and a folded napkin to resemble a wreath hanger complete this holiday place setting.

"Oh Christmas Tree" Trims

You can have any style of Christmas tree you like when you paint the little green trees on purchased white ornaments using glass paints and glitter.

WHAT YOU NEED
Purchased white matte-finish Christmas ornament • Old towel • Glass paints in desired colors of green • Paintbrush • Crafts glue with fine tip • Fine glitter in desired colors of green, gold, copper, and silver • ½-inch wide green satin ribbon for bow • Narrow ribbon for hanging

WHAT YOU DO
1. Be sure the ornament is clean and dry. Place the ornament on the towel to keep it from rolling. You will be painting one side at a time.
2. Referring to the diagrams, right, as inspiration, paint the tree shapes as desired on one side of the ornament. Let dry. Repeat for the other sides of the ornament.
3. Use the fine tip on the crafts glue to add highlights to the trees and dust with glitter. Let dry.
4. Thread the ribbon through the top of the ornament and tie a bow. Add the narrow ribbon for hanging.

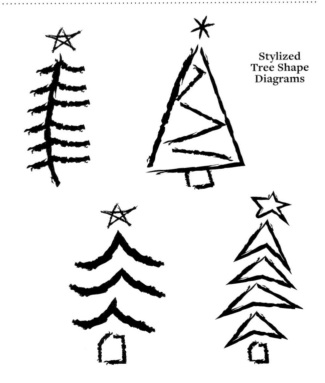

Stylized Tree Shape Diagrams

Wool tweed combines with decorative buttons to create little pillow sachets to hang on doorknobs, on the tree, or to give as a special gift.

Tiny Woven Pillow Sachets

Wool tweed fabric in seasonal green colors is cut into tree shapes and stitched into tiny pillows for a perfect hostess gift.

WHAT YOU NEED

For three trees

¼ yard of green wool tweed fabric • Poly fiberfill stuffing • Scissors • Thread to match fabric • Flat buttons in assorted colors of green • ¾-inch wide ribbon • Sachet filler such as balsam

WHAT YOU DO

1. Enlarge and copy the template, right, and cut out. For each pillow, cut 2 pieces from wool, reversing one.
2. With right sides together, stitch a ⅜-inch seam all around the tree shape leaving the bottom open for turning. Turn and press.
3. Fill the tree with fiberfill and sachet and sew opening closed. Do not overfill.
4. Sew the buttons to the front of the tree. Tie a bow and secure at the top. Add a hanging loop if desired.

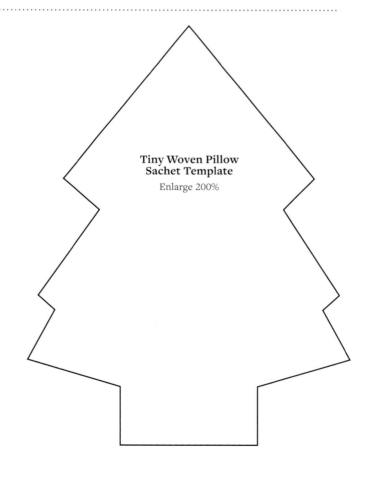

Tiny Woven Pillow Sachet Template
Enlarge 200%

Rickrack Christmas Stocking

Snippets of rickrack mimic the design on the fabric on these fun stockings that hang on mismatched dresser pulls.

WHAT YOU NEED
Tracing paper • Pencil • ½ yard of green print flannel fabric for body • ½ yard of interfacing for lining • ¼ yard coordinating printed flannel for cuff • ¼ yard coordinating printed flannel for toe/heel • Jumbo rickrack in green and white • Scissors • Matching sewing thread

WHAT YOU DO FOR EACH STOCKING
1. Enlarge and trace templates on page 64, and cut out. Use the stocking template to cut a front and a back, reversing one of the shapes. Repeat for the lining. Cut the cuff from coordinating fabric. Cut 2 heel and 2 toe pieces from coordinating printed flannel.

2. Turn under edge on toe and heel pieces and press. Topstitch in place on stocking front and back, matching stocking edges.
3. With right sides together, stitch cuff on two short and one long side. Clip corners, turn, and press. Topstitch rickrack to bottom edge of cuff, or as desired.
4. Stitch stocking pieces with right sides together, leaving top edge open, using ⅜-inch seam. Clip curves. Turn right side out.
5. Stitch lining pieces with right sides together, using ⅜-inch seam. Trim the seam close to stitching to reduce bulk in stocking. Insert lining inside turned stocking, keeping top straight edges even. Pin right side of cuff to inside lining of stocking and stitch, leaving cuff ends open. Turn cuff to outside of stocking and press.
6. From the rickrack make a hanging loop and tack to inside of stocking.

Choose flannel fabrics in three or four different coordinating prints to make these festive stockings. Use jumbo rickrack trim or other fun trim such as pom-poms to finish the cuffs.

Rickrack Stockings Templates

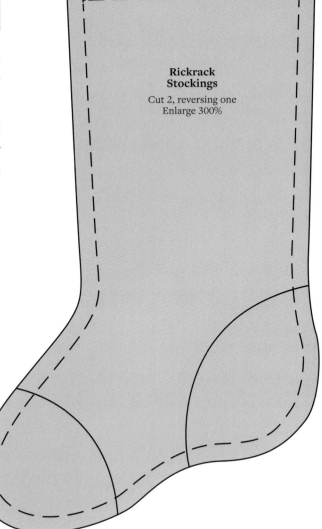

Fold

Rickrack Stockings Cuff
Cut 2
Enlarge 300%

Rickrack Stockings
Cut 2, reversing one
Enlarge 300%

Rickrack Heel
Enlarge 300%

Rickrack Toe
Enlarge 300%

Festive Green Yarn Balls

Textured yarn in shades of green are wrapped around foam balls for a quick and easy decorating accent.

WHAT YOU NEED

For 8 balls

3-inch foam balls such as Styrofoam • 1 skein of green and white textured yarn • Straight pins • Small holiday star and word stickers • Shallow bowl or basket

WHAT YOU DO

1. Cut a long length of yarn and secure the end with a pin into the foam ball. Wrap the yarn around and around until the ball is completely covered. Secure with pin.

2. Place the star and word stickers on the ball. Group the balls in a shallow basket or bowl for display.

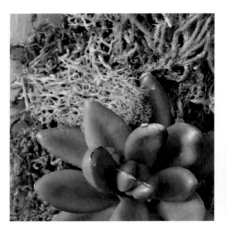

Hues of Green Succulent Wreath

Succulent green plants are grouped with green ornaments for a beautifully textured wreath for the holidays.

WHAT YOU NEED
10-inch foam wreath form such as Styrofoam • Artificial succulent plants • Natural moss (available at crafts stores) • Hot-glue gun and glue sticks • Small green ornaments • 1½-inch wide green burlap-style ribbon for hanging

WHAT YOU DO
1. Plan the design by laying out the artificial succulent plants and ornaments on the wreath. Using a hot-glue gun and glue sticks, attach the artificial succulents and ornaments around the wreath form. TIP: If succulents are on a wire, pierce the wire through the wreath form to help secure to wreath.
2. When all pieces are in place, attach small bits of moss using the hot-glue gun around the wreath until you can no longer see the wreath form.
3. Loop the ribbon around the top of the wreath for hanging.

A variety of natural succulents can be displayed in rustic terra-cotta bowls for a quick centerpiece that evokes warmth and natural beauty. Add a few green ornaments around the outside for a festive touch.

Let the lovely shades of green in natural or artificial succulent plants become the color palette for your Christmas decorating.

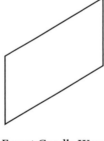

**Forest Candle Wrap
Template**

Forest Candle Wrap

Tiny pieces of tissue paper, in all shades of green, line up side by side to create stunning candle holders.

WHAT YOU NEED

Tissue paper in assorted green colors • Glass pillar candle holder • Decoupage medium such as Mod Podge • Foam crafts brush • Natural twine • Adhesive star sticker with jewel • Hot-glue gun and glue sticks

WHAT YOU DO

1. Using the template, above left, as a guide, cut parallelogram shapes out of tissue paper. Set aside.
2. Be sure the glass pillar is clean and dry. Coat the outside of the glass pillar with decoupage medium. Place parallelogram shapes onto candle holder, overlapping to form different colors and patterns. Cover the entire pillar with the shapes.
3. When the entire pillar is covered, seal with a light layer of decoupage medium. Let dry. Wrap the twine around the top of the pillar and tie a knot at the front. Attach the sticker and star at the knot with hot glue.

Never leave a burning candle unattended.

Lime and String Pomanders

Little bits of green string wrap around whole cloves for this new take on an old holiday favorite.

WHAT YOU NEED
8 fresh limes • Skewer • Whole cloves • Green bakers' twine

WHAT YOU DO
1. Referring to the photo, opposite, use a skewer to mark the holes on the limes where you want to place the whole cloves. Insert the cloves into the holes.
2. Use the string to wind around the cloves to make designs. Place in a shallow bowl for display.

Note: Fruit will last about 2 weeks.

Sparkling Green Pinecones

Natural pinecones are painted green and dusted with shades of green glitter to make a lovely display.

WHAT YOU NEED
Natural pinecones • Metallic spray paint in desired shades of green • Fine glitter in desired shades of green • Small paintbrush • Crafts glue • Water

WHAT YOU DO
1. Be sure the pinecones are clean and dry. Lay pinecones in a well-ventilated area and spray with desired shades of green paint. Let dry.
2. Mix equal parts of glue and water and lightly brush on the painted pinecones. Dust with glitter. Let dry.

Glorious Garlands

Decorate your home for the holidays with these festive Christmas garland and swag ideas. Try draping the garlands on banisters, mantels, windows, and doorways to transform your everyday spaces into a winter wonderland.

Lovely Felt Leaf Swag

Layers and layers of felt in all colors of green come together for a stunning window swag.

WHAT YOU NEED
Nonwoven felt such as National Nonwovens in a variety of green hues • Hot-glue gun and glue sticks • Scissors • 1 yard of 1-inch wide ribbon

WHAT YOU DO
1. Trace the leaf template, right, and cut out. Use the template to cut out leaf shapes from the desired colors of green felt. You will need about 80 leaves for a 36-inch garland.
2. For each leaf, fold the leaf over, lengthwise, and secure at the bottom with a dot of hot glue (indicated by circle on template). Glue a row of leaves together, at the bottoms, staggering and lining the straight edges up. Make two rows. Glue the rows together to form the garland.
3. Cut the ribbon in half. Fold each in half again and glue to the ends of the garland for hanging.

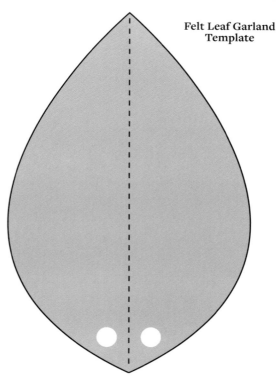

Felt Leaf Garland Template

Burlap and Lace Garland

Bits of burlap, wood beads, and lace scraps combine for a lovely little textured garland to hang for the holidays.

WHAT YOU NEED

Small square wood beads with holes • Scraps of burlap • Scraps of cream-color lace • Needle • Heavy weight thread • 1 yard of ½-inch wide natural twill tape • Scissors

WHAT YOU DO

1. Cut strips from the burlap pieces and set aside. Cut short lengths from the lace pieces and set aside.
2. Thread the needle with the heavy thread using the length of thread desired. Start the garland by threading one of the wooden beads onto the thread and tie to secure, leaving a tail of thread for hanging.
3. Accordion fold the twill tape and thread onto the heavy thread. Tie on burlap and lace pieces as desired, continuing to thread the beads, twill tape, burlap, and lace until the desired length is reached.
3. Add a wooden bead at the end to secure in place.

Shimmering Poinsettias

Gently curved creases bring life to pearlescent cardstock and vellum to create a garland of stunning paper poinsettias.

WHAT YOU NEED

Pearlescent cardstock • Vellum • Bone folder • Hot-glue gun and glue sticks • 4-foot piece of string • Red cardstock • Paper punch • White florist's wire

WHAT YOU DO

1. Enlarge and copy the leaf template, right, and cut out. Draw around the leaf template onto the cardstock and vellum. You will need about 30 leaves to make a 24-inch garland.

2. Score the leaf shapes on the gray dotted line a scoring tool. Hot-glue folded leaves to string.

3. Punch out little red berries from the red cardstock. Place the florist's wire between two punched berries and glue them together. Twist the wires into clusters of three and hot-glue to the leaf backs.

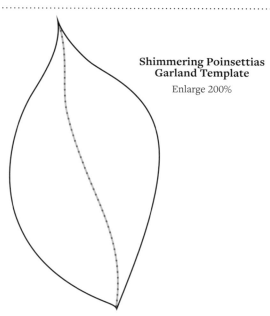

**Shimmering Poinsettias
Garland Template**

Enlarge 200%

Folded Fanfare

Solid, patterned, and metallic cupcake liners combine into a crazy-quilt-inspired garland.

WHAT YOU NEED

Cupcake liners in desired sizes, prints, and colors • Stapler • Crafts glue • Narrow ribbon • Scissors

WHAT YOU DO

1. Plan the design of the garland by laying out the liners on a flat surface. Fold six regular-size liners in half. Staple them together in overlapping rows to form an upside-down rounded triangle. Staple in the back so the front "flap" hides the staple. Layer on folded mini liners where desired. Use dots of glue to hold the flaps down.

2. Continue folding and stapling liners into upside-down triangles. Staple the assembled triangles together until you have the desired length. Embellish ends with ribbon.

Vineyard Garland

Wine corks, little bunches of grapes, and copper beads combine to make a simple garland with a beautiful bouquet.

WHAT YOU NEED
Wine corks • Little bunches of artificial grapes • Copper beads • Drill and small drill bit • Dental floss • Large needle

WHAT YOU DO
1. Plan the design by laying out the components on a flat surface. Use the drill bit to drill small holes in the center of the wine corks. Set aside.
2. Cut dental floss to desired length and thread the needle. Thread the corks, bunches of grapes, and beads in desired order. Tie at ends.

Nature Findings Garland

Let nature guide you to create a lovely textured garland for your tree or mantel.

WHAT YOU NEED
Pinecones • Acorns and other nature findings • Drill and small drill bit • Fine wire

WHAT YOU DO
1. Plan the design of the garland by laying the elements needed in the order desired. Use a drill and drill bit to make small holes in the pinecones, acorns, and other nature findings.
2. Make a loop at the end of the wire. Thread the pinecones and other natural items on the wire. Make a loop at the final end to secure.

Painted Beads and Blocks Garland

Metallic silver cording and ribbon join painted blocks and Christmas-red beads to make a colorful, jewel-like string.

WHAT YOU NEED
Square wood beads with holes • Aqua crafts paint • Paintbrush • Red and silver beads • Silver ribbon • Narrow silver cording • Scissors

WHAT YOU DO
1. Paint the wood beads with the aqua paint. Let dry.
2. Plan the garland by placing the elements side by side in desired order on a flat surface. Cut the silver cording to the desired length. Thread the blocks and beads onto the silver cording, leaving space between for the tied ribbons.
3. Cut the silver ribbon into short pieces. Tie the ribbons between the blocks and beads using one knot. Trim the ends.

Sweet Candy String

Sugar candies line up to make a super sweet and simple little garland for a tiny tree.

WHAT YOU NEED
Candies such as gumdrops, fruit slices, and jelly beans • Waxed dental floss • Large needle • Bowl of warm water

WHAT YOU DO
1. Plan the garland by placing the candies side by side in desired order on a flat surface.
2. Thread the needle with the floss and dip the needle into water. Thread the candies in the desired order, dipping the needle in the water to avoid sticking. Tie off ends.

Note: Garland will last for the entire season and can be frozen to keep for next year in sealed plastic container. Do not eat.

Giving Garland

Each tiny envelope is decorated with jewels and paper tape and connected with one another for a garland that will hold little Christmas gifts.

WHAT YOU NEED
Small envelopes • Paper punch • Stickers • Metallic paper tape such as Washi tape • Narrow silver ribbon • Silver and gold tissue paper

WHAT YOU DO
1. Lay the envelopes in a line with the top flap open. Punch a hole on both sides right under the flap.
2. Decorate the envelopes with metallic paper tape and stickers as desired.
3. Cut the silver ribbon into 10-inch pieces. Thread through the holes and tie a knot to secure. Trim the ends of the ribbon. Cut small pieces of tissue paper and place inside the envelopes.

Little envelopes are strung together with narrow silver ribbon to make a garland of pretty gift holders. Fill them with gift cards, tickets, folded money, or hand-written notes.

Visions of Sugar Plums

Make the season magical with pastel hues and sugar-sweet projects
that will keep visions of Christmas dancing in their heads.

Shimmering glitter clings to the inside of clear teardrop ornaments to make dazzling trims for your holiday tree.

Sparkling Glitter Trims

So easy to make and lots of fun to do, these iridescent ornaments can be made in any colors that you chose.

WHAT YOU NEED

Teardrop-style glass ornaments with removable tops • Decoupage medium such as Mod Podge • Water • Small bowl • Spray bottle • Fine glitter in desired colors • Old egg carton • Narrow ribbon

WHAT YOU DO

1. Be sure the ornaments are clean and dry. In a small bowl mix together 2 tablespoons of decoupage medium and 1 cup of water. Pour into spray bottle.

2. Remove the tops from the ornaments. Carefully spray the water mixture into the inside of the ornaments. Shake desired colors of glitter into the inside of the ornament and swirl around until desired effect is achieved. Turn the ornament upside down and rest in the egg carton. Let dry for at least 4 hours or overnight.

3. Place the top back on the ornament and add a ribbon for hanging.

Mercury Glass Candy Dishes

Castaway clear dishes become pieces of art when they are magically transformed into beautiful mercury glass dishes to hold holiday sweets.

WHAT YOU NEED
Small glass dishes (from flea markets or thrift shops) • Mirror spray paint such as Rust-Oleum Mirror Effect spray paint • Spray bottle filled with 1 part white vinegar and 1 part water • Paper towels • White cupcake liners • Small bowl • Food coloring • Water • Crafts glue

WHAT YOU DO
1. Be sure the glass dishes are clean and dry. Mist entire outside of glass dish with vinegar/water mixture. While wet, spray paint outside of glass dish with mirror-effect spray paint. While wet, mist outside of glass dish again with vinegar/water mixture. Let dry for 2 minutes then lightly blot with a paper towel.
2. Continue the same process several times until desired effect is reached. Let dry completely.
3. In a small bowl mix water and desired color of food coloring. Dip the tops of the cupcake liners into the colored water. Lay out to dry.
4. Use crafts glue to glue the liners to the inside of the dishes. Fill with candy.

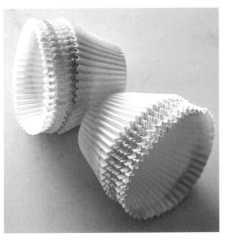

Mirror spray paint turns plain glass dishes into beautifully textured mercury glass. Dyed cupcake liners create delicate little holders for sweet sugarplum candies.

Pearl and Bead Candy

Wooden beads become sugar-like candy when they are glittered and strung on yards and yards of pearls.

WHAT YOU NEED
Wooden beads • Pastel-colored craft paint in desired colors • Fine glitter in the same colors as the paint • Decoupage medium such as Mod Podge • Foam crafts brush • String pearl beads (small enough to fit through wooden beads) • Hot-glue gun and glue sticks

WHAT YOU DO
1. Paint the wooden beads with the pastel crafts paint. Let beads dry.
2. Use a foam crafts brush to apply decoupage medium around the beads. Sprinkle the beads with glitter of the same color. Let dry.
3. String the wood beads onto the string of pearl beads. Secure on both sides of the bead with a dot of hot glue.

Felt Pinwheel Trim

Roll up some felt strips and string them with buttons on bakers' twine to mimic a pretty string of candy.

WHAT YOU NEED
Nonwoven felt such as National Nonwovens in pastel colors • Scissors • Hot-glue gun and glue sticks • Buttons in pastel colors • Bakers' twine or thin ribbon in pastel colors • Large needle

WHAT YOU DO
1. Cut ½-inch wide strips of felt in three pastel colors; length depends on the size of the pinwheel you would like to create.
2. Stack all three strips atop of one another and secure together with a small amount of hot glue. Wrap the felt around in a circle, securing with hot glue at the end.
3. Use a needle and bakers' twine to string pinwheels, attaching buttons between the pinwheels. Tie at the ends.

Felt Pinwheel Package Trim

Use little felt pinwheels and a white muffin liner to make a sweet package topper.

WHAT YOU NEED
Small white paper muffin liner • Hot-glue gun and glue sticks • Bakers' twine • Wrapped package

WHAT YOU DO
1. Make felt pinwheel candy as in 1 and 2 of the Felt Pinwheel Trim, page 91. Hot-glue the piece inside a white cupcake liner. Let dry.
2. Wrap the twine around the package and tie a knot on the top. Hot-glue to the top of the wrapped package.

Swirl Ornaments

Metallic paint swirls inside clear glass ornaments to make dreamlike colors and shapes.

WHAT YOU NEED
Round clear glass ornament with removable tops • Metallic crafts paint • Water • Paper cup • Decoupage medium such as Mod Podge (optional) • Paintbrush (optional) • Fine glitter (optional)

WHAT YOU DO
1. Mix 10 parts craft paint to 1 part water. Make several colors that when mixed make a pretty color.
2. Drop several colors of the diluted paint into the ornament. Swirl paint around inside of ornament, adding more paint as necessary, until entire ornament is covered in paint. Let dry upside down in a paper cup until totally dry. Colors will blend together as they drip dry. When dry, put top back on ornament.
3. If desired, use a paintbrush and decoupage medium to paint swirls on the outside of the ornament. Dust with glitter.

Almost like magic, the goblet that holds the pastel candy canes and sugary gumdrops disappears behind the sweet Christmas treats.

Candy Cane Centerpiece

Pretty pastel candy canes rest on a straight-sided vase as a pink goblet holds sugary gumdrops.

WHAT YOU NEED
Straight-sided vase large enough to hold goblet • Stemmed goblet to fit inside the vase • Wide print ribbon in pastel colors • Pink pom-pom trim • Double-stick tape • Scissors • Pastel candy canes • Gumdrops

WHAT YOU DO
1. Be sure the vase and goblet are clean and dry. Cut a piece of ribbon to fit around the vase. Use double-stick tape to secure the ribbon to the middle of vase. Use double-stick tape to secure the pom-pom trim at the top of the ribbon.
2. Place the goblet into the glass vase. The top of the goblet should be slightly taller than the vase. Starting at one side of the vase, rest the candy canes all around the vase, arranging by color as desired. Readjust as needed to fit.
3. Place the gumdrops in the top of the goblet.

Cross-Stitch Ribbon Candy

Tiny candy-colored cross-stitches are worked onto plastic canvas and then bent to look like sweet ribbon candy.

WHAT YOU NEED
6 colors of pastel color embroidery floss • Cross-stitch diagram • 1 12×18-inch sheet of 7-count clear plastic canvas for cross-stitch such as Darice • Large bead

WHAT YOU DO
1. Cut the plastic canvas, leaving 152×19 holes. Using 3 strands of floss, work cross stitches following the cross-stitch diagram, right.
2. When complete, using all 6 strands of one color of floss, create the ribbon shape by sewing through the stitched piece in an accordion shape (indicated by black dots on diagram: 6 holes, 20 holes, 20 holes, 20 holes, 20 holes, 20 holes, 20 holes, 20 holes, 6 holes). At the bottom, attach a large bead. Sew back up through the ribbon using the same holes (6-20-20-20-20-20-20-20-6). Tighten and tie the ends together.

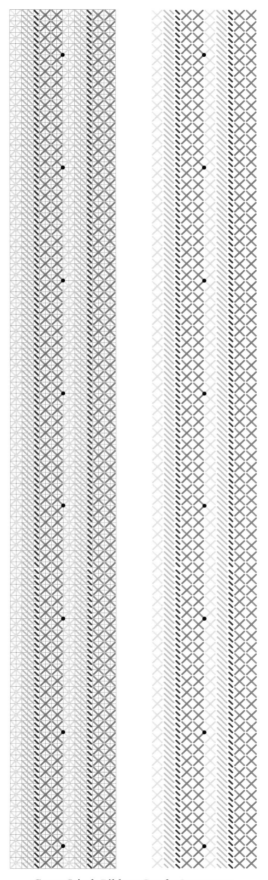

Cross Stitch Ribbon Candy Ornament
152×19

Embroidered Winter Cards

Pretty colors of metallic embroidery floss are worked on white wool to create visions of a winter wonderland that make perfect holiday greetings.

WHAT YOU NEED
Small pieces of cream wool fabric • Transfer paper • Metallic embroidery floss in pastel colors • Embroidery needle • Scissors • Pastel color scrapbook papers • Blank white greeting cards • Glue stick • Double-stick tape

WHAT YOU DO
1. Cut the white wool to measure at least 2 inches larger all the way around the chosen template. Copy the chosen template, below, and transfer to the white wool using transfer paper. Use 3 plies of the metallic thread to work embroidery stitches using the Straight Stitch, French Knot, or other stitches if desired. (See page 160 for Stitch Diagrams.) Trim any loose threads on the back of the cards.

2. Trim the wool to fit the blank card. Fringe the edges of the wool about ½ inch from the edge of the wool. Cut a piece of coordinating scrapbook paper for the front of the card. Secure the papers together with glue stick. Use double-stick tape to adhere the wool to the scrapbook paper.

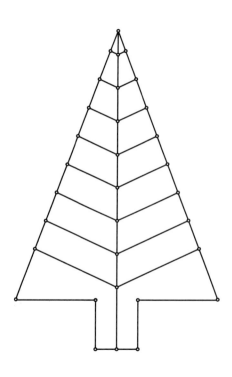

Embroidered Winter Cards Templates

Use metallic pastel embroidery floss and simple stitches to make greeting cards that will surely be kept and enjoyed year after year.

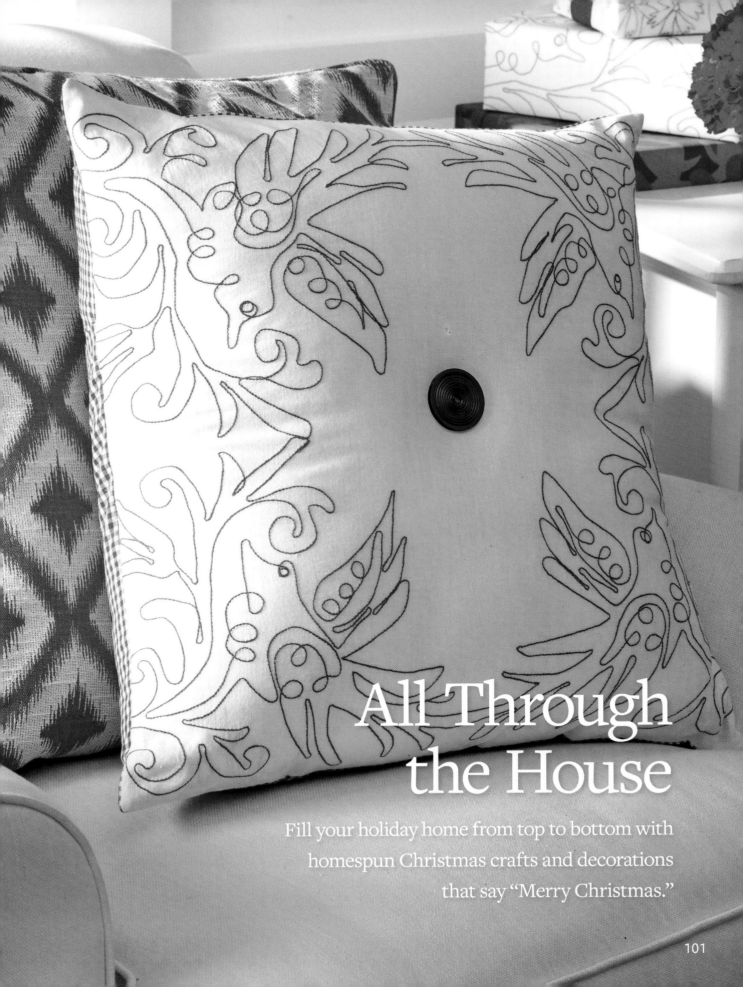

All Through the House

Fill your holiday home from top to bottom with homespun Christmas crafts and decorations that say "Merry Christmas."

Fresh Apple Wreath Welcome

A trip to the produce section for a few apples and Key limes yields big style on a welcoming wreath for your home. Use wire or wood picks to secure apples and Key limes to a floral foam wreath (with an attached plastic backing). Hot-glue or wire pinecones and boxwood on the outer edge to fill in the gaps. To change the color scheme, use Granny Smith apples and lemons, or use faux fruit for a wreath you can use year after year. This wreath is even versatile enough to use as a centerpiece; lay it on the table, and add a pillar candle or hurricane in the center.

Oh Christmas Tree

Make your holiday tree the center of attention using traditional trims with a touch of woodland charm. Decorate the tree with handmade ornaments, yellowish green balls, bells, and floral sprays that stand out against the dark green boughs. Add reds for a pop of holiday color to match the fresh apple wreath. Sew some simple-stitch stockings, and wrap pretty packages to add to the charm of this holiday setting.

Use the woodland-style moose and reindeer head templates in varying sizes for ornaments, decorative art pieces, and package tie-ons.

Woodland Ornament

Display a little trophy or two by adhering a reindeer or moose motif to wood plaques and showcasing them as Christmas trims.

WHAT YOU NEED
Cardstock • White felt • Wood plaque cutout • Fast-drying crafts glue such as Beacon 3-in-1 adhesive • Fine cording

WHAT YOU DO
1. Enlarge and trace the desired template, right and opposite, onto cardstock and cut out for a template. Cut 2 pieces of felt and a piece of cardstock, all larger than the template.
2. Glue a piece of felt and cardstock together. Place the template on the cardstock and trace around it using a pencil; cut out with scissors. Glue the template cutout, felt side up, onto the second piece of felt. Trim excess felt. Fold back the felt at the neck and glue onto the wood plaque cutout for ornament.
3. On the back, add a cord for hanging or glue to package if using as package trim.

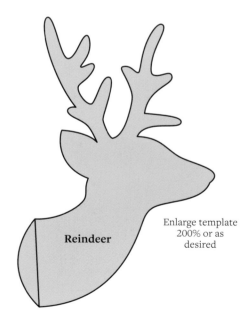

Reindeer

Enlarge template 200% or as desired

Small silhouettes work well for decorative art pieces and gift tags. Or print larger profiles of the templates onto white paper, cut them out, and adhere them to plain-paper packages.

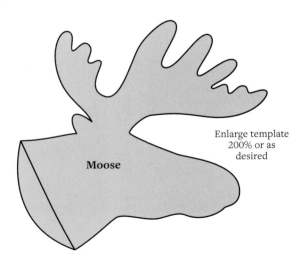

To make a package tie-on, simply copy the desired template onto green paper. Cut out and adhere to a white tag. Use a stamp or stencil to add the greeting.

Woodland Art

MATERIALS
Frame • Small piece of wool for inside frame • Metal tag or charm • Fabric glue • White felt • Scissors

DIRECTIONS
1. Enlarge and trace the desired template, opposite and right, in the desired size for the chosen frame, and cut out from white felt. Cut the wool to fit inside the frame. Use fabric glue to glue the felt to the wool.
2. Add the metal tag or charm at the bottom of the wool piece for interest.
3. Frame the finished piece.

Moose

Enlarge template 200% or as desired

Natural Nuances Pines

Craft wintry pines by covering plastic foam cones with snow-dusted cardstock petals.

WHAT YOU NEED
Kraft wrapping paper • Double-stick tape • 8½×11-inch cardboard-color cardstock • Plastic-foam cones such as Styrofoam, 12-inch, 15-inch, and 18-inch cones • Hot-glue gun and glue sticks • Aerosol snow

WHAT YOU DO
1. Wrap paper around cones, creating a point. Attach to cone using tape. Using the template, below, cut leaves from cardstock. Roll leaves using your finger or a pencil for a slight outward curve.
2. Starting at the bottom of each cone attach the top of the leaf to the cone using hot glue. Continue attaching rows of leaves, overlapping slightly, until you are a few rows from the top. On the top two rows, roll leaf sides in using your finger or a pencil, and adhere them to the tree top. Spray with snow.

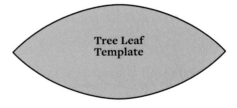

Tree Leaf Template

Organic Impressions Ornaments

Delightfully detailed, these snowy white ornaments take just minutes to make. Press air-dry clay onto cookie molds to imprint natural motifs and seasonal shapes.

WHAT YOU NEED
Air-dry clay such as DAS clay • Clay roller and clay mat • Cookie and springerle molds • Round-style toothpick • Round cookie cutter • Clay scissors • Wire rack • Fine-grade sandpaper

WHAT YOU DO
1. Lightly roll out a small piece of air-dry clay, place it over a cookie mold, and continue to roll out the clay to an even thickness. Gently peel the clay away from the mold and check to make sure all impressions from the mold are clear. Using a round-style toothpick, make a hole in the clay for hanging.
2. Use a round cookie cutter to trim around circular designs; using clay scissors, trim excess from other shapes.
3. Let the ornaments dry on a wire rack, turning each shape over periodically. When dry, smooth any rough edges using fine-grade sandpaper.

Shades of Green Stocking

Trendy houndstooth fabric and green velvet combine to make a happy little stocking for Santa to fill.

WHAT YOU NEED
• Tracing paper • Pencil • ⅔ yard houndstooth fabric • ⅔ yard lining fabric • ½ yard green velvet fabric • Scissors • Matching thread

WHAT YOU DO
1. Enlarge and trace templates, right, onto tracing paper; cut out templates. Using the template, cut out two stockings (reverse one of them) each from houndstooth and lining fabrics. Using the template cut cuff from velvet fabric. For cut binding, cut and piece a velvet bias strip to measure 2¼×27 inches. For a hanging loop, cut a 1⅔×7-inch bias fabric strip.

2. With houndstooth right sides together and using a ¼-inch seam allowance sew stocking front to back, leaving top edge open. Clip curves, turn right side out, and press. Sew lining pieces in same manner, increasing seam allowance to ⅜ inch through the ankle and foot; do not turn right side out.

3. With right sides together and using a ½-inch seam allowance sew bias binding strip to cuff's curved edge. Fold binding over seam allowance to wrong side of cuff and press. Stitch in the ditch between cuff and binding. Trim excess binding.

4. Fold the hanging loop strip in thirds lengthwise and press. Topstitch along long edges. Trim length to 6 inches. Fold in half to form hanging loop; sew short edges together. Slip lining into stocking body, matching side seams. Pin end of hanging loop inside lining at heel seam, matching raw edges. Stitch around top of stocking.

5. Lay cuff right side down with curved edge away from you. Starting at the short straight edge, roll cuff into a manageable bundle. With right side of cuff facing the lining, place curved edge of cuff next to hanging loop, matching raw edges. Using a ½-inch seam allowance, stitch cuff to stocking, unrolling bundle as you sew. The cuff will overlap about 6 inches from where you began sewing. Pull the cuff up and fold down over the stocking.

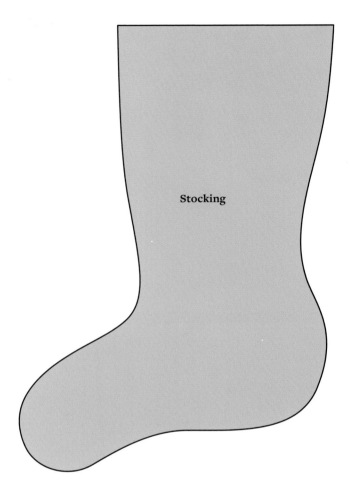

Stocking

Enlarge all templates 400%

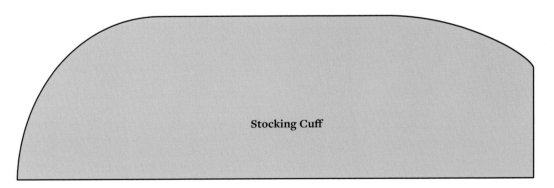

Stocking Cuff

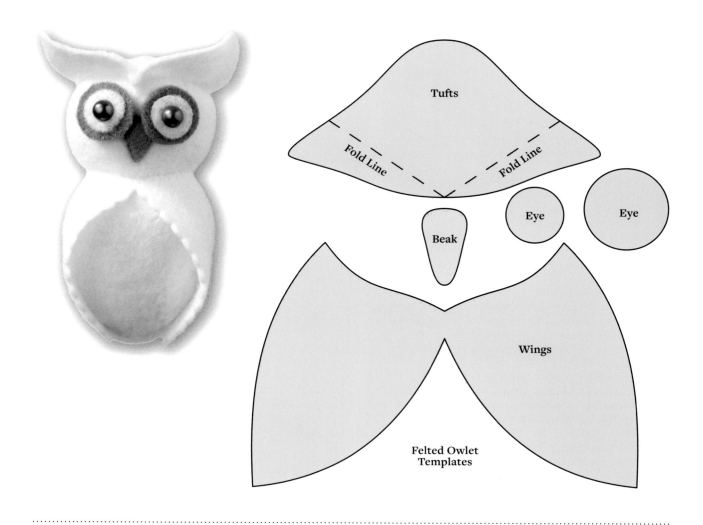

Give a Hoot Felted Owlet

Make cute needle-felt owlets to hang on the tree. Or stuff them into stockings sewn from an interesting mix of plush, woven, and embroidered fabrics.

WHAT YOU NEED
2-inch plastic-foam ball such as Styrofoam (for head) • 2½-inch plastic-foam egg such as Styrofoam (for body) • Fast-drying crafts glue such as Beacon 3-in-1 Adhesive • Felt: white, green, and brown • Needle-felting tool • Pinking shears • Self-adhesive pearl halves

WHAT YOU DO
1. Using a knife, shave one end of the ball and one end of the egg to create a flat area for the forms to meet. Attach the flat ends together using a toothpick and glue to form the head and body.
2. Place the body on a piece of felt and cut the felt piece large enough to wrap around both the head and body. Placing the felt on the front center of the egg, needle-felt by pouncing the felting tool until the felt fibers begin to mesh with the egg. Start in a small area and keep the holes closely spaced together. Continue needle-felting, working outward and around the body.
3. Once the egg-shape portion is done, begin in the center of the ball shape and move outward and around. Trim excess felt at the top and bottom, continuing to needle-felt until the entire form is covered. Needle-felt the area where the head and body meet to create an indentation.
4. Trace the template, above, and cut out the wings from felt. Trim the wing front edges using pinking shears. Needle-felt the wings to the indented neck area. Add crafts glue to the straight back edge of each wing and adhere each wing to the body to create a cupped shape.
5. Trace the template, above, and cut out the tufts from felt. Apply glue to the center front and fold together. Let dry. Place the tufts on the owlet head and needle-felt the tufts to the head, but do not needle-felt the front tuft areas.
6. Cut out the eyes and beak from felt, using the templates above. Needle-felt the beak in place. Needle-felt the eyes in the center of the face. Glue the pearl pupils to the eyes.

Petal
Template

Mistletoe Sprig Package Trim

The topper on this package is like a special little gift all its own.

WHAT YOU NEED
Lightweight fusible interfacing • 2 shades of green velvet • Pinstripe background rubber stamp • Lightweight fusible adhesive • Silver metallic embroidery floss • Small white felted balls • 20-gauge wire • Florist's tape • Fast-drying crafts glue such as Beacon 3-in-1 Adhesive

WHAT YOU DO
1. Cut a piece of fusible interfacing and both colors of velvet slightly larger than the rubber stamp. Fuse interfacing to the wrong side of the lighter color velvet, following manufacturer's instructions.
2. Lay the rubber stamp on the work surface, rubber side up. Place the fused velvet, pile side down, on top of the stamp. Mist the interfacing side of the velvet with water and, using firm pressure, iron the fabric for 10 to 15 seconds. Continue misting and ironing until the interfacing is dry and you see the stamp pattern through the interfacing. Following

manufacturer's instructions, attach the fusible adhesive to the darker velvet.
3. With wrong sides together, fuse velvet pieces together. Using the petal template, cut 9 petals for each gift topper or trim.
4. Dab crafts glue on the top of a petal and pinch the sides together. Hold until it sets. Apply glue to the second petal, place on top of the first petal, and pinch sides together. Hold until it sets. Add glue to the top edge of the third petal and glue to the previously joined petals. Let dry, then trim the excess velvet from the top edges. Repeat to create two more bunches of petals for each gift topper or trim.
5. Using a needle and floss, pull floss through a felted ball. Pull the needle through the top of one bunch of petals so the felted ball rests inside the petals. Tie a knot and cut off excess floss. Repeat with two more balls to form three bunches of petals. Using one end of a 5-inch length of wire, gather the clusters together at the top. Cover the remaining wire with florist's tape, twirling to adhere. Shape into a hanging loop.

Picture-Perfect Packages

Make your package presentation as meaningful as the gift inside. Wrap the gift with printed paper and make a memorable gift tag by inserting a snapshot into a small frame. Tie the photo and a cute charm to the present with ribbon.

Use vintage fabric to make a festive pillow. But before you stitch it up, use the fabric as inspiration for custom gift wrap. Lay the fabric on a color copier and print out pages to use for wrapping presents.

Festive Vintage Pillow

Use that lovely vintage fabric you found in Grandma's trunk for a pillow and matching gift wrap.

WHAT YOU NEED

Vintage linen such as redwork or embroidered pillowcases • Coordinating fabric for back of pillow • Scissors • Matching thread • Poly fiberfill • Coordinating button • Needle

WHAT YOU DO

1. Plan the design of the pillow by letting the design on the fabric guide the size and shape of the pillow. Cut the fabric to the desired size. Cut a piece of coordinating fabric the same size for the back of the pillow.
2. With right sides together, stitch the back and the front of the pillow together leaving an opening for turning.
3. Turn the pillow right side out and stuff lightly with poly fiberfill. Do not overstuff. Sew opening closed.
4. Use a needle and thread to sew a button in the center of the pillow.

Fun and Festive Christmas Tabletop

Favorite colors and motifs of the season all come together in this fun little table setting for the holidays.

To make the Envelope-Style Folded Napkin:
Place a cloth napkin diagonally on a flat work surface. Fold the bottom point up, diagram 1, aligning it with the top point to form a triangle, diagram 2. Fold the left and right corners in, diagram 3, so the points meet in the center. Fold the left and right sides to the center again, diagram 4. Fold the bottom edge up to the center of the "diamond," diagram 5. Fold the top down, diagram 6, forming the envelope flap, diagram 7. Use a Santa medallion sticker or other sticker on the envelope napkin flap.

To make the Cookie Cutter Favor:
For the reindeer cookie cutter, trace around a metal reindeer-shape cookie cutter (the kind without a handle and covered top) onto scrapbooking paper; cut out slightly smaller than the traced line. Press the reindeer cutout into the cookie cutter. If needed, glue the edges of the reindeer to hold it in place.

To make the Bottle Glass:
For the bottle, wrap a strip of scrapbook paper around the bottle and add a sticker in the middle. Place a printed paper straw inside the bottle.

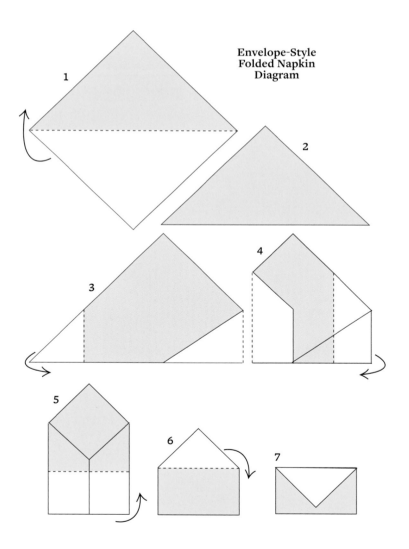

Envelope-Style Folded Napkin Diagram

Create an easy and playful tabletop that can be pulled together with a few basics; a red place mat, a white plate, and a white napkin folded to look like an envelope that holds a letter to Santa. Then make a cookie cutter reindeer favor and a fun milk bottle drinking glass.

Nibbles & Sips

Dish up holiday cheer with these effortless appetizers. Many can be made ahead of time and others cook unattended in your slow-cooker. Start the party with hot dips, stuffed veggies, festive drinks, and more.

Shrimp-and-Bacon-Stuffed Baby Potatoes

Tiny new potatoes become a clever vessel to hold the cheesy shrimp and bacon filling.

WHAT YOU NEED

14	tiny new potatoes (about 1¼ pounds)
2	tablespoons Dijon mustard
1	tablespoon olive oil
2	teaspoons Old Bay seasoning
1	7- to 8-ounce package frozen, peeled, cooked shrimp, thawed, drained, and chopped
½	of an 8-ounce package cream cheese, softened
1	cup shredded Gouda cheese (4 ounces)
5	slices bacon, crisp-cooked, drained, and crumbled
¼	cup snipped fresh chives (optional)

WHAT YOU DO

1. Preheat oven to 425°F. Cut potatoes in half lengthwise. Using a small melon baller or a very small spoon, scoop out potato pulp, leaving ¼-inch-thick shells. Cut a thin slice from the bottom of each potato half so it stands upright. Place potatoes, cut sides up, in a 15×10×1-inch baking pan.

2. In a small bowl combine mustard, oil, and 1 teaspoon of the Old Bay seasoning. Brush insides of potato shells with mustard mixture. Bake about 30 minutes or until potatoes are tender.

3. Meanwhile, for filling, in a small bowl combine shrimp, cream cheese, Gouda cheese, bacon, and the remaining 1 teaspoon Old Bay seasoning. Spoon filling into potato shells, mounding slightly.

4. Bake for 12 to 15 minutes more or until filling is heated through and cheese is melted. Serve warm or at room temperature. If desired, garnish with chives.

Makes 28 appetizers.

Bacon-Cheddar Potato Dip

The addition of cream cheese transforms mashed potatoes into a party dip that tastes just like twice-baked potatoes. Scoop with halved mini peppers.

WHAT YOU NEED

2¼	pounds Yukon gold or other yellow-flesh potatoes, peeled and quartered
4	slices hickory- or applewood-smoked bacon
1	8-ounce tub cream cheese spread
1	cup shredded sharp cheddar cheese (4 ounces)
½	cup sour cream
2	tablespoons milk
¼	cup chopped green onions (2)
¼	teaspoon garlic salt
	Potato chips, sweet peppers, green onions, or other desired dippers

WHAT YOU DO

1. In a covered large saucepan cook potatoes in enough boiling, lightly salted water to cover for 15 to 20 minutes or until tender; drain.

2. Meanwhile, in a large skillet cook bacon over medium heat until crisp. Remove bacon and drain on paper towels. Crumble bacon; reserve 1 tablespoon of the crumbled bacon for topping.

3. In a large bowl combine the remaining crumbled bacon, cream cheese spread, ¾ cup of the cheddar cheese, the sour cream, milk, green onions, and garlic salt. Press cooked potatoes through a ricer* onto the cheese mixture; stir gently to combine. Spoon potato mixture into a 1½- or 2-quart slow cooker. Cover and cook on low-heat setting about 2 hours or until heated through (160°F).

4. Sprinkle with the remaining ¼ cup cheddar cheese and the reserved bacon. Serve immediately or keep warm, covered, on warm- or low-heat setting for up to 2 hours. Serve dip with potato chips or other dippers.

Makes 48 servings.

*Tip: If you don't have a ricer, mash the potatoes with a potato masher until fluffy.

Bacon, Blue Cheese, and Potato Dip: Prepare as directed, except substitute 1 cup crumbled blue cheese (4 ounces) for the cheddar cheese. Serve with barbecue-flavor potato chips or celery sticks instead of sour cream-and-onion-flavor potato chips or pepper wedges.

Cheesy Skillet Artichoke Dip

No dippers needed! Mini rolls that bake on top of hot artichoke dip are perfect for scooping. Serve the dip and rolls right from the skillet.

WHAT YOU NEED

1   15- to 16-ounce package frozen white dinner rolls, thawed (12 rolls)
1   8-ounce package cream cheese, softened
1   8-ounce carton sour cream
¼   cup milk
1   8-ounce package shredded Italian blend cheeses (2 cups)
2   14-ounce cans artichoke hearts, drained and chopped
3   cups chopped fresh baby spinach
½   cup sliced green onions (4)
2   cloves garlic, minced
1   tablespoon butter, melted
1   tablespoon grated Parmesan cheese

WHAT YOU DO

1. Divide each roll into two portions. Shape each portion into a small ball, pulling edges under to make a smooth top. Place rolls 2 to 3 inches apart on a floured sheet of parchment paper or waxed paper. Lightly cover and let rise for 1 to 1½ hours or until nearly double in size.
2. Preheat oven to 375°F. In an extra-large mixing bowl beat cream cheese with an electric mixer on medium to high for 30 seconds. Add sour cream and milk; beat until combined. Beat in 1½ cups of the shredded cheeses. Stir in artichokes, spinach, green onions, and garlic. Transfer artichoke mixture to an oven-going extra-large skillet, spreading evenly. Sprinkle the remaining ½ cup shredded cheeses over dip.
3. Bake for 15 minutes. Remove skillet from oven.
4. Arrange rolls with sides touching on top of hot dip (rolls will fit snugly and cover entire surface). Lightly brush roll tops with melted butter. Sprinkle rolls with Parmesan cheese. Bake for 15 to 20 minutes more or until rolls are golden and dip is hot. Let stand for 10 minutes before serving. **Makes 24 servings.**

Hot Reuben Dip

Take the fixings for the classic grilled sandwich—sauerkraut, cheese, and corned beef—and create this tasty hot dip.

WHAT YOU NEED

1   14- to 16-ounce can sauerkraut, rinsed and well drained
1½   cups shredded regular cheddar cheese (6 ounces)
1½   cups shredded regular Swiss cheese (6 ounces)
6   ounces corned beef, chopped (about 1¼ cups)
1   cup mayonnaise
    Pita chips, baguette-style French bread slices, and/or toasted party rye bread

WHAT YOU DO

1. Preheat oven to 350°F. For dip, pat sauerkraut dry with paper towels. In a large bowl combine sauerkraut, cheddar cheese, Swiss cheese, corned beef, and mayonnaise.
2. Spoon dip into an ungreased 9-inch quiche dish or 1½-quart casserole, spreading evenly.
3. Bake, uncovered, about 25 minutes or until dip is heated through and edges are bubbly. Serve dip with pita chips, baguette slices, and/or rye bread. **Makes 15 servings.**
Microwave Directions: Prepare as directed, except spoon dip into an ungreased 1½-quart microwave-safe casserole. Microwave, uncovered, on 100-percent power (high) for 5 to 6 minutes or until heated through, stirring twice. Serve as directed.

Individual Italian Quiches

These miniature quiches make a great first course and couldn't be easier to make. Just roll the dough into balls and press into muffin cups; then add the cheesy filling.

WHAT YOU NEED

1   recipe Pastry Dough
⅔   cup packaged shredded Italian blend cheeses
½   cup finely chopped red sweet pepper (1 small)
¼   cup finely chopped pancetta or prosciutto
1   tablespoon thinly sliced green onion
1½   teaspoons all-purpose flour
¼   teaspoon dried Italian seasoning, crushed
⅛   teaspoon salt
⅛   teaspoon ground black pepper
3   eggs
1¼   cups half-and-half, light cream, or whole milk
    Chopped pancetta or prosciutto, crisp-cooked (optional)
    Snipped fresh parsley (optional)

WHAT YOU DO

1. Preheat oven to 375°F. Shape chilled Pastry Dough into twenty 1½-inch balls. Place each ball into a 2½-inch muffin cup. Press dough into bottoms and up sides of muffin cups; set aside.

2. In a medium bowl combine cheeses, sweet pepper, the ¼ cup pancetta, the green onion, flour, Italian seasoning, salt, and black pepper. Divide cheese mixture evenly among pastry shells.

3. In the same bowl beat together eggs and half-and-half. Pour egg mixture over filling in each pastry shell.

4. Bake about 20 minutes or until filling is set. Let stand in muffin cups for 5 minutes. Using a small sharp knife, gently loosen edges of the shells from the sides of muffin cups; remove from the cups. Cool slightly; serve warm. If desired, garnish with additional crisp-cooked pancetta and/or parsley. **Makes 20 mini quiches.**

Pastry Dough In a medium bowl stir together 2 cups all-purpose flour and ½ teaspoon salt. Using a pastry blender, cut in ¾ cup cold butter, cut up, until pieces are pea size. Sprinkle 1 tablespoon ice water over part of the flour mixture; toss gently with a fork. Push moistened dough to side of bowl. Add additional ice water, 1 tablespoon at a time, until all of the flour mixture is moistened (¼ to ⅓ cup total). Gather mixture into a ball, kneading gently until it holds together. Wrap in plastic wrap and chill for at least 1 hour.

Sugared Bacon-Wrapped Smokies

Coating the bacon-wrapped sausages in brown sugar before baking gives them a crunchy glaze. The combination of sweet, smoky, and salty is irresistible!

WHAT YOU NEED

    Nonstick cooking spray
1   16-ounce package small cooked smoked sausage links
15   slices bacon, each cut crosswise into thirds
¾   cup packed brown sugar

WHAT YOU DO

1. Preheat oven to 350°F. Line a 15×10×1-inch baking pan with foil; lightly coat foil with cooking spray. Set aside.

2. Wrap each sausage link with a bacon piece, overlapping ends of the bacon piece. Press ends to seal or secure with wooden toothpicks.

3. Place brown sugar in a large plastic bag. Add several bacon-wrapped sausages to bag. Seal bag; gently shake bag to coat sausages with brown sugar. Place sausages in prepared pan. Repeat with remaining bacon-wrapped sausages and brown sugar.

4. Bake, uncovered, about 30 minutes or until the bacon browns. Serve immediately. **Makes 6 servings.**

Make-Ahead Directions Do not preheat oven. Prepare as directed through Step 3. Cover pan with foil and chill for up to 24 hours. To serve, preheat oven to 350°F and continue as directed in Step 4.

Jamaican Jerk Chicken Sliders with Pineapple Salsa

Bring an island twist to your holiday table with these easy sliders. Chicken thighs, slow-simmered in a blend of coffee, molasses, and lime juice are served in mini buns and topped with a tongue-tingling pineapple salsa.

WHAT YOU NEED
2   tablespoons Jamaican jerk seasoning
2   tablespoons olive oil
1   teaspoon kosher salt
¾   teaspoon ground black pepper
3½   pounds bone-in chicken thighs, skin removed
1   cup brewed coffee
¾   teaspoon finely shredded lime peel (set aside)
3   tablespoons lime juice
2   tablespoons molasses
4   cloves garlic, minced
     Several dashes bottled hot pepper sauce
1½   cups finely chopped fresh pineapple
¼   cup chopped green onions (2)
¼   cup chopped red sweet pepper
2   tablespoons snipped fresh cilantro
1   fresh jalapeño chile pepper, seeded and finely chopped* (optional)
16   slider buns or small round dinner rolls, split and, if desired, toasted

WHAT YOU DO
1. In a small bowl combine jerk seasoning, oil, salt, and black pepper. Coat chicken with seasoning mixture. Place chicken, bone sides down, in a 3½- or 4-quart slow cooker.
2. In a small bowl combine coffee, 2 tablespoons of the lime juice, the molasses, garlic, and hot pepper sauce. Pour mixture over chicken.
3. Cover and cook on low-heat setting for 7 to 8 hours or on high-heat setting for 3½ to 4 hours.
4. Using a slotted spoon, remove chicken from cooker. When chicken is cool enough to handle, remove meat from bones; discard bones. Using two forks, pull chicken apart into shreds. Return shredded chicken to cooker. If using low-heat setting, turn to high-heat setting. Cover and cook about 30 minutes more or until heated through.
5. Meanwhile, for salsa, in a medium bowl stir together pineapple, green onions, sweet pepper, cilantro, jalapeño pepper (if desired), the remaining 1 tablespoon lime juice, and lime peel.
6. To serve, use the slotted spoon to spoon chicken mixture onto bottoms of buns. Top with salsa; replace tops of buns. **Makes 16 sliders.**
***Tip:** Because chile peppers contain volatile oils that can burn your skin and eyes, avoid direct contact with them as much as possible. When working with chile peppers, wear plastic or rubber gloves. If your bare hands do touch the peppers, wash your hands and nails well with soap and warm water.

Bacon and Cheese Deviled Eggs

A bit of bacon and hint of cheddar liven up classic deviled eggs.

WHAT YOU NEED
12   hard-cooked eggs
½   cup mayonnaise
1   tablespoon honey mustard
¼   teaspoon salt
¼   teaspoon ground black pepper
4   slices bacon, crisp-cooked and crumbled
2   tablespoons shredded sharp cheddar cheese
     Bacon, crisp-cooked and crumbled (optional)
     Chopped green onion (optional)

WHAT YOU DO
1. Halve eggs lengthwise and remove yolks. Set whites aside. Place yolks in a small bowl; mash with a fork. Stir in mayonnaise, honey mustard, salt, and pepper. Fold in 4 slices crumbled bacon and the cheese.
2. Stuff egg white halves with yolk mixture. Cover and chill until serving time (up to 24 hours). If desired, garnish with additional bacon and green onion.
Makes 24 servings.

Cinnamon-Pumpkin Toddy

The stick cinnamon garnish doubles as a stirrer, so guests can mix the whipped cream into this warm spiced drink. Shown on page 116.

WHAT YOU NEED
5   cups water
½   cup pure maple syrup
⅓   cup canned pumpkin
1   cup rye whiskey or bourbon
½   cup apple-cinnamon or cinnamon schnapps
1   recipe Cinnamon Whipped Cream
    Ground cinnamon and/or stick cinnamon

WHAT YOU DO
1. In a 3½- or 4-quart slow cooker combine the water, maple syrup, and pumpkin.
2. Cover and cook on low-heat setting for 3 to 4 hours or on high-heat setting for 1½ to 2 hours. Stir in rye whiskey and schnapps.
3. Ladle into mugs. Serve with Cinnamon Whipped Cream and garnish with ground cinnamon or stick cinnamon.
Makes 8 servings.
Cinnamon Whipped Cream In a chilled mixing bowl beat 1 cup whipping cream, 2 tablespoons sugar, and 1 teaspoon ground cinnamon with chilled beaters of an electric mixer on medium until soft peaks form (tips curl).

Raspberry Mojito Punch

If you like, combine the ingredients in Step 1 in the punch bowl up to 24 hours ahead of time and chill until needed. When ready to serve, add the carbonated water and ice.

WHAT YOU NEED
¼   cup sugar
¼   cup lightly packed fresh mint leaves
3   cups cold water
1½ cups white rum
1   12-ounce can frozen raspberry juice blend concentrate, thawed
½   cup lime juice
1½ cups carbonated water, chilled
    Ice cubes
    Fresh raspberries and/or fresh mint (optional)

WHAT YOU DO
1. In a punch bowl combine sugar and the ¼ cup mint. Using the back of a wooden spoon, lightly crush mint by pressing it against the side of the bowl. Add the cold water, the rum, juice concentrate, and lime juice, stirring until sugar is dissolved.
2. Slowly pour carbonated water down the side of the bowl; stir gently. Add ice cubes. If desired, garnish with raspberries and/or fresh mint. **Makes 8 servings.**
Virgin Raspberry Mojito Punch Prepare as directed, except omit rum and increase carbonated water to 3 cups.

Zesty Popcorn Snack Mix

Store this savory snack mix at room temperature in a tightly covered container for up to 2 days. For longer storage, use the rice cakes instead of the popcorn.

WHAT YOU NEED
6   cups unsalted popped popcorn or 6 cups broken unsalted rice cakes
3   cups corn chips or coarsely broken tortilla chips
3   cups mini pretzel twists
1½ cups dry roasted cashews or peanuts
¼   cup butter, melted
2   tablespoons Worcestershire sauce
1   tablespoon chili powder
2   teaspoons ground cumin
1   teaspoon garlic salt
½   teaspoon cayenne pepper
½   cup snipped dried apricots

WHAT YOU DO
1. Preheat oven to 250°F. In a large roasting pan combine popcorn, corn chips, pretzel twists, and cashews. In a small bowl stir together butter, Worcestershire sauce, chili powder, cumin, garlic salt, and cayenne pepper. Pour butter mixture over popcorn mixture, tossing to coat.
2. Bake about 30 minutes or until the coating on snack mix begins to darken slightly, stirring occasionally. Spread snack mix on a large piece of foil and let cool. Stir in dried apricots. **Makes 18 servings.**

Candles All Aglow

Let shimmering candlelight make your holiday glow
with the spirit of the season.

Paper Lace Candle Stands

Clear glass cake stands make beautiful candle holders when they are embellished with paper lace.

WHAT YOU NEED

Tape measure • Pedestal-style plate • Decorative paper border punch • Cardstock or parchment paper in desired colors • Scissors • Double-stick tape • Pillar candles

WHAT YOU DO

1. With a tape measure, measure around the edge of the pedestal plate that will be used. Cut the cardstock or parchment paper into a strip that fits around the edge of the cake plate, piecing the strip as needed.
2. Use the decorative paper punch to punch the design into the cardstock or parchment paper. Wrap the strip around the pedestal and secure with double-stick tape.
3. Place candles on pedestal.

Never leave a burning candle unattended.

All dressed up for the holidays, vintage canning jars are adorned with purchased beaded bracelets. A floating candle finishes the simple candle centerpiece.

Ombre Candles

Subtle colors of wax are layered to make little holiday candles.

WHAT YOU NEED
Unwrapped crayons in desired colors broken into small pieces • Soy wax • Paper cups • Cooking spray such as Pam • Plastic spoons for mixing • Candle wicking

WHAT YOU DO
1. To create the first layer, in a paper cup, melt ⅓ to ½ cup soy wax and broken crayon bits in microwave 30 seconds at a time, stirring between warming times. Continue until soy wax and crayons are completely melted. Note: Watch wax carefully; do not overheat
2. Spray another paper cup with cooking spray. Place the wick in the bottom of the paper cup and pour the first layer of wax into the cup. Let dry.
3. Create remaining layers by repeating step 1, using different shades of crayons each time. Add layers until the desired look is achieved. Let dry completely.

Beaded Mason Jar Candles

Purchased bracelets are wrapped around vintage blue Mason jars for a sparkling effect.

WHAT YOU NEED
Vintage Mason jars • Beaded elastic bracelets • Water • Floating candles

WHAT YOU DO
1. Be sure the jars are clean and dry. Pull the elastic bracelets around the tops of the jars.
2. Fill the jars with water and add floating candles.

Never leave a burning candle unattended.

Simple wood posts are transformed into trendy candle holders for the holidays. A rainbow of glitter colors is dusted at the bottom of each candle for a modern and festive look.

Blocks of Color Candles

Wood posts are cut, drilled, and glittered to make modern candle holders for inside or outside light.

WHAT YOU NEED

4×4-inch wood post • Table saw • Sandpaper • 1½-inch spade bit (wide enough to accommodate tea light) • Decoupage medium such as Mod Podge • Foam brush • Glitter • Tea light candles

WHAT YOU DO

1. Cut a 4×4-inch wood post to desired height. Sand rough edges. Drill a hole, approximately ½-inch deep in the top center of the wood post, deep enough to accommodate the tea light.

2. Brush decoupage medium onto the bottom of the wood block using a foam brush, thinning the glue as you move the brush toward the top.

3. Dust with glitter. Let dry. Place a tea light candle in the hole at the top.

Never leave a burning candle unattended.

Whether right-side up or upside-down, beautifully shaped goblets reflect the light of the season as they hold pretty little tea lights.

Candy Treasures Candles

Hidden under clear goblets, candy of all kinds adds color and playful texture to the candle centerpiece.

WHAT YOU NEED
Clear goblets in a variety of shapes and sizes • Clear cake stand • Christmas candies • Tea lights

WHAT YOU DO
1. Be sure the glass pieces are clean and dry. Fill the goblets with candy. Invert and place on the cake stand.
2. Place a tea light on the top (bottom) of the goblet.

Never leave a burning candle unattended.

Goblet Candles

Combine glass vessels for a stunning candle holder.

WHAT YOU NEED
Clear straight-sided glass vase • Goblet to fit inside the vase • Small vintage ornaments • Tea light candle

WHAT YOU DO
1. Be sure the glass vessels are clean and dry. Carefully place the small ornaments in the bottom of the vase.
2. Lower the goblet into the glass vase, making sure the goblet rests evenly on the ornaments. Place the tea light into the goblet.

Never leave a burning candle unattended.

Pierced Tin Candles

Delicate flickers of soft light come through the beautiful shapes on these tin candles.

WHAT YOU NEED
Decorative sheet metal (available at home stores) •
Tin snips • 220 grit sandpaper • Clamps • Bronze spray
paint, suitable for metal • 20 gauge wire • Pliers

WHAT YOU DO
1. Using tin snips, cut a section of decorative sheet metal
6×14 inches or cut to size of candle. Sand rough edges with
220 grit sandpaper.
2. Wrap metal in a circle and secure with a clamp on the
top and the bottom. Starting at the bottom, "sew" it shut
using wire continuing up to the top then back down to the
bottom, tightening with pliers as you go.
3. Twist the wires together at the bottom with wires and
trim. Spray paint the bottom of the candle wrap with
bronze spray paint, graduating the spray paint as you move
up the candle. Let dry.

Wrap it Up Candles

Beads, charms, and wraps combine to make lovely embellished holiday candles.

WHAT YOU NEED
Pillar candles in desired colors • Wraps such as
bakers' twine and leather cording • Charms • Beads
• Straight pins

WHAT YOU DO
1. Plan the design by laying out the beads and charms in
the order to be strung.
2. Cut the twine or leather, leaving plenty of length for
wrapping. String the beads and charms onto the twine or
cording. Pin in place at the back of the candle. Add another
layer of twine and charms if desired.

Never leave a burning candle unattended.

Painted Nature Findings Candle

Add some color to nature's beautiful shapes with just a touch of metallic paint.

WHAT YOU NEED
Metallic paints in desired colors • Nuts in the shell such as pecans • Slice of wood large enough to hold candles • Pillar candles • Greenery • Pinecones

WHAT YOU DO
1. Paint the nuts with the metallic paints. Let dry.
2. Arrange the candles on the slice of wood. Add greenery, painted nuts, and pinecones around the candles.

Never leave a burning candle unattended.

Nature Inspired Candle

Bits of nature are combined with a floating candle for a naturally beautiful look.

WHAT YOU NEED
Glass vase • Natural sticks • Floral putty • Small rocks • Water • Fresh cranberries • Floating candle

WHAT YOU DO
1. Measure the sticks and cut them to fit so they extend from the top of the vase. Secure them at the bottom with floral putty.
2. Place rocks around the sticks at the bottom of the vase.
3. Pour water into the vase. Add the cranberries and the floating candle.

Never leave a burning candle unattended.

Package Deal

This year put the pretty back into your package presentation with a wrap that is just as beautifully thought-out as the handsome gift you give.

Cosmetic Purse and Gift Bag

So quick to make and so useful and fun to use, you can make these little bags in any fabric you chose.

WHAT YOU NEED

Finished purse is 4×7-inches
9×9-inch piece of fabric • 9×9-inch piece of lightweight iron-on interfacing • 7-inch zipper in matching color of fabric • Scissors • Matching thread • Straight pins • Purchased fabric flowers or other trim • Needle

WHAT YOU DO
1. Fuse the interfacing to the fabric. Note: When you are making the bag, you will be treating the two fused fabrics as one piece.
2. Cut 2 pieces of the interfaced fabric to measure 8×5 inches. Open the zipper, and with right sides together, sew one side to each long side of the fabric using a ½-inch seam.
3. Leaving the zipper open, with right sides together, pin and then baste the other three sides of the bag together using ½-inch seams, catching just the end of the zipper in the seam. Stitch in place; remove pins and basting threads.
4. Tack the trim on the front of the bag. Close the zipper.

For the Wrap
Choose a gift bag that coordinates with the fabric that you used for the cosmetic purse. Use fabric instead of tissue to cushion the gift in the bag. Tie a cork letter to the bag and a sticker on the front of the bag.

Letter Monogram Framed Art

A sprig of laurel surrounds a single letter for a personalized framed gift.

WHAT YOU NEED
Paper • Pencil • Ornate plaster frame • Tightly woven neutral fabric large enough to fit frame • Permanent black marker • White crafts paint • Gold crafts paint • Foam brush

WHAT YOU DO
1. To prepare the frame, paint the frame white and let dry. Paint the bottom and up one-third of the frame with gold paint. Let dry. Set aside.
2. Cut a piece of paper the same size as the inside of the frame. Plan the design on paper first. For the letter, use a stencil or a printout of the letter in a favorite font or plan to draw the letter freehand. Transfer to the fabric.
3. Enlarge or reduce the size of the laurel leaf template, above, and transfer onto the fabric around the letter, reversing one side. Use the black permanent marker to color in the design. Frame the fabric in the frame.

For the Wrap
Choose a wide gold ribbon and tie it diagonally around the frame using double-stick tape to secure.

Front

Mason Jar Jewelry

Mason jars are a popular go-to supply for crafters, but when they are broken and tumbled they make stunning jewelry.

WHAT YOU NEED

Vintage blue or clear Mason jar (or to order precut and polished drilled glass pieces or complete kits, see Sources page 160.) • Plastic bag • Paper bag • Hammer • Tumbler for smoothing glass or stones • CORDLESS dremel drill and diamond-coated drill glass drill bit • Small plastic dish • Water • Goggles • 21 gauge square silver wire • Bail or round nose pliers • Beads or stones with holes • Chain, wire, or cording

WHAT YOU DO

1. Wearing goggles, put the Mason jar into a strong plastic bag and then into a paper bag. Use a hammer to gently tap the jar until it breaks into small pieces.
2. Put the pieces into the tumbler following directions on tumbler until glass is smooth on all edges.

3. Place the smoothed glass piece in the dish and add just enough water to cover the piece. Wearing goggles, use a CORDLESS dremel drill with a diamond coated drill bit to drill a hole in one end of the glass piece. Note: DO NOT use a drill with a cord—this could result in electric shock.
4. Cut a piece of square wire 8 inches long. Insert into the glass hole and fold in half. Using bail-making or round nose pliers, pinch at the top of the glass piece. Fold the wire over the pliers one or two times to create the bail. Wrap remaining wire around the stem of the wire under the bail pliers and above the glass. See illustration, above.
5. Bring the wire around to the front of the glass and make swirls. Add small beads or rocks to the wire if desired.
6. Place a chain, wire, or cording in the bail for necklace.

For the Wrap

Choose a brown paper box and decorate with aqua paper tape such as Washi tape. Use alphabet letters to spell out the word "JOY" on the front of the box.

Buttoned-Up Crochet Hat

WHAT YOU NEED
3.5 ounce cotton yarn in desired color • Size I crochet hook • Large button • Scissors

WHAT YOU DO

For the Hat Body:

Row 1: CH 3. SL ST to join. Ch 1. Ch 9 HDC into center. SL ST to join.

Row 2: CH 2. Ch 2 HDC in each stitch around. Join with SL ST.

Row 3: CH 2. HDC in first stitch, 2 HDC in next stitch, repeating pattern around. Join with SL ST.

Row 4: CH 2. HDC in first stitch, 2 HDC in next stitch, repeating pattern around. Join with SL ST.

Row 5: CH 2. HDC in each ST around hat. SL ST to join.

Rows 6-12: CH 2. PS in every other ST around hat (To create PF: YO, insert hook in CH 1 space, YO insert hook in same CH1 space, YO, insert hook in same CH1 space, pull through all loops on hook. CH 1.).

Rows 13-16: HDC in each ST around hat. SL ST to join and fasten off.

For the Hat Band:

Row 1: CH 13.

Rows 2-3: CH 1. HDC in each stitch.

Row 4: CH 1. HDC in each stitch. Fasten off.

Wrap band around the rim of the hat. Secure in place by sewing button on band. Trim all lose ends.

For the Wrap

For the crochet package toppers you will need 3.5 ounce skeins of acrylic yarn in desired colors, size H crochet hook, and purchased felted balls.

To make the crochet toppers, make a slip knot and slide it onto the crochet hook. Chain stitch a row to desired length. Chain three stitches. Work one double crochet stitch in every chain stitch until you reach the end of the row. Fasten off. Repeat for as many colors as desired. Wrap chain around in a ball shape. Wrap yarn around the package. Glue crochet toppers and felted balls onto the package. Add a gift tag.

CROCHET ABBREVIATIONS

CH	chain
SL ST	slip stitch
ST	stitch
HDC	half double crochet
YO	yarn over
PS	puff stitch

So simple to make and yet so trendy and fun, this crochet hat is the perfect gift for any age. Make it in the color of yarn that suits that special person on your holiday gift list.

Who's Got the Button?

Sweet Lollipop Wrap

Gilded Monogram

*Simple additions to a simply
wrapped package such as a
few colorful buttons, a sweet
lollipop, a paper snowflake,
or a personalized initial letter,
make these packages stand
out under the Christmas tree.*

Wrap it Up!

Let your presentation be as pretty as the gift with simple ideas that will let you wrap it up in no time! Just a button here or a paper snowflake there will add that little special something to a plainly wrapped gift. So gather your crafting tools and enjoy making your gifts the ones that they'll want to open first.

Who's Got the Button?

Polka-dot paper is accented with Christmas-hue buttons for a very Merry Christmas package.

WHAT YOU NEED
Polka-dot paper • Buttons to fit inside the dots of the paper • Crafts glue • Christmas tag

WHAT YOU DO
Wrap the box with the polka-dot paper. Glue the buttons on the dots. Add the tag.

Sweet Lollipop Wrap

Diagonally wrap some twill tape around a striped package and tuck in a colorful lollipop for a super-sweet presentation.

WHAT YOU NEED
Diagonal stripe paper • Natural-color twill tape • Sticker • Double-stick tape • Lollipop to match paper

WHAT YOU DO
Wrap the gift with the paper. Wrap the twill tape around the box at a diagonal; secure with double-stick tape. Place the sticker over the twill tape. Tuck the lollipop under the twill tape.

Gilded Monogram

The big initial gives a clue to the intended recipient of this package. Have fun monogramming packages for every family member. The monogram is a wooden letter transformed with gold leaf. Paint or paper tape works too.

WHAT YOU NEED
Wood cutout • Artist's brush or foam brush • Gilding adhesive • Gold leaf sheet • Double-stick tape • Wide ribbon or bands of paper • Glitter tape

WHAT YOU DO
1. Brush the wood cutout with gilding adhesive; let dry until tacky. Press the gold leaf sheet against the wood cutout. Rub gently over the backing paper, then lift off the paper. Let dry for 15 minutes. Brush off excess gold leaf around the edges.
2. Layer a package with wide ribbons or bands of paper and a narrower band of glitter tape. Tape the wood cutout to the package.

Snowflake Flurry

Snowflake Flurry

Recognize this snowflake paper? It is a coffee filter all dressed up with pearlescent paint.

WHAT YOU NEED
White basket-style coffee filter • Paintbrush • Watercolor paint in pearlescent white • Double-stick tape • Ribbon

WHAT YOU DO
1. Paint one side of the coffee filter with the watercolor paint; let dry. Fold the coffee filter in half, then in half again, and in half two more times so it forms an elongated cone shape. Trace the template, below, onto cardstock and cut out for a template.
2. Trace around the template onto the folded coffee filter. Use sharp scissors to cut the design into the folded coffee filter. Unfold and flatten the coffee filter, revealing the snowflake. Tape or glue ribbon in an X shape to a gift box lid. Tape the snowflake on top.

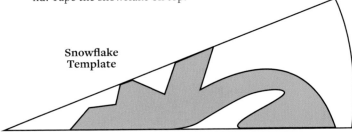

Snowflake Template

Place on open edge of folded filter

Metallic Glamour

Initial Impression

Two-Bead Tassel

Wooden Wonder

Metallic Glamour

A cluster of pom-poms made from metallic yarns serves as a fluffy bow on the package.

WHAT YOU NEED
Pom-pom maker • Metallic yarns in three complementary colors • Glitter string • Double-stick tape

WHAT YOU DO
Use the pom-pom maker and metallic yarns to make one large and two medium pom-poms. Tie a wrapped package with glitter string, creating an asymmetrical cross with three vertical and three horizontal strands; tape in back. Tape pom-poms where the glitter yarns intersect.

Initial Impression

Kids will have fun helping to make the glittered letter tag. It's made from air-dry clay, and the "monogram" was done with a cookie cutter.

WHAT YOU NEED
Roller or rolling pin • Air-dry clay • Letter cookie cutter • Needle tool or toothpick • Linerbrush • Decoupage medium • Gold glitter • String

WHAT YOU DO
1. Roll out clay to the desired tag size and about ¼ inch thickness. Use the cookie cutter to cut a letter from the center (do not cut all the way through the clay). Use the needle tool or toothpick to make a hole in the upper left corner. Let dry.
2. Brush decoupage medium on the letter indentation. Sprinkle with glitter, shake out excess glitter, and let dry. Thread a string or ribbon through the hole to attach to a wrapped package.

Two-Bead Tassel

Gold leaf works its magic on a wooden ball tassel that strikes just the right note to set against vintage sheet music.

WHAT YOU NEED
Paintbrush • Gilding adhesive • Large and medium wooden beads • Gold leaf sheet • Embroidery floss

WHAT YOU DO
1. Brush the gilding adhesive on the large bead, leaving some areas uncoated. Let dry until tacky. Press the gold leaf onto the bead; use fingers to gently press loose pieces into place.
2. Fold a piece of embroidery floss in half. Knot the folded end, leaving a loop at the top. Slide the medium bead, then the large bead, onto the loose ends of the embroidery floss. Knot the loose ends, leaving enough floss to pull strands apart to create a fringed end. Attach bead tassel to ribbon.

Getting Dotty

Getting Dotty

With sequins and few dots of glue, plain wrapping paper gains a polka-dot pattern and loads of personality. Keep the look classic with silver and gold sequins, or sprinkle on bright colors for confetti-inspired fun.

WHAT YOU NEED
Sequins in gold and silver • Quick-setting gel glue • Scissors • Gold metallic ribbon

WHAT YOU DO
Glue the sequins to a wrapped package in a random design. Cut some in half to create the effect of dots running off the edge of the paper. Tie a bow using the gold ribbon around the package.

Wooden Wonder

A wooden doily serves as a medallion to bring dimension and charm to a package wrapped in kraft paper. A circle punched from cardstock delivers a custom holiday message.

WHAT YOU NEED
Quick-setting gel glue • Wood cutout • 2½-inch circle punch • Pearl-finish cardstock • Rubber stamp and ink

WHAT YOU DO
Glue the wood cutout to the front center of a package. Punch a circle from cardstock. Stamp the design on the punched circle. Glue it to the wood cutout.

Gold-Tipped Feathers

Gold-Tipped Feathers

Liquid gilding brushed onto the tips of white feathers starts this package off in an elegant manner.

WHAT YOU NEED
Paintbrush • White crafts feathers • Liquid gilding: gold • Paper cutter or scissors • Embossed scrapbook paper • Double-sided tape • Ribbon with a shimmery finish • Tag

WHAT YOU DO
1. Brush the tips of the feathers with liquid gilding. Stand the feathers upright; let dry.
2. Cut the scrapbook paper so it's slightly narrower than a wrapped package, then wrap it around the package; tape in back. Wrap ribbon around the package, knotting in front. Tuck the feathers and a tag under the ribbon.

Good As Gold

For classic elegance, a gold-and-white color scheme can't be beat. A patterned paper starts things off, though you could also use solid white. The asymmetrically placed spray-painted floral pick layered atop glitter paper, offers a change from the usual ribbon.

WHAT YOU NEED
Gold glitter paper • Double-stick tape • Gold spray paint • Floral leaf pick • Short piece of cream ribbon • Crafts glue • Scissors

WHAT YOU DO
1. Cut a 5×12-inch strip of glitter paper. Use scissors to notch one end. Place the glitter paper strip on a wrapped package.
2. Spray-paint the floral leaf pick; let dry. Tie the ribbon around the floral pick stem; glue it onto the glitter paper strip.

Tasseled Flair

A tissue paper tassel strikes a "let's party" note on a holiday package. Try it on a birthday present too.

WHAT YOU NEED
Tissue paper in pink, cream, gold Mylar, and two shades of green • Cutting mat • Rotary blade • Straightedge • Glitter string • Ribbon • Jingle bells

WHAT YOU DO
1. Layer five sheets of tissue paper on the cutting mat. Using the rotary blade and straightedge, cut the stack into a 5×12-inch rectangle. Fold the stack in half to 6 inches long. Cut slits in the tissue paper, spaced ½ inch apart and stopping short of the top. Unfold the tissue paper and roll into a cylinder. Twist the middle to form a loop. Secure ends with glitter string or yarn.
2. Thread the looped tassel onto ribbon and tie the ribbon around a wrapped package. Embellish the package with jingle bells threaded onto glitter string.

Sequined Strands

Want razzle-dazzle? Sequins threaded on glitter yarn offer it up with minimal effort.

WHAT YOU NEED
Glitter yarn • Sequins in various colors and sizes • Tape

WHAT YOU DO
1. Cut the yarn long enough to wrap around a wrapped package several times. String sequins onto the yarn. Tape one end of the yarn to the back of the package; wrap the string around the package several times, moving and spacing sequins so they appear on the front. Tape in back.
2. Cut another piece of yarn. Wrap it around the center of the package and the sequined strands, taping in back.

Good As Gold

Give your gift wrap some sparkle with gold-tipped feathers, gold glitter paper, glittered jingle bells, and shimmering sequins.

Tasseled Flair

Sequined Strands

Peel-and-Stick Panache

Tree Topping

Earthy Allure

Poinsettia Topper

Peel-and-Stick Panache

Glitter tapes produce a sparkly pattern on the package. Tassels are also cleverly made from the same tapes. Vary the tape colors to fit your holiday scheme and transform any solid-color paper.

WHAT YOU NEED
Glitter tape in various colors, such as gold, red, and pink • Flexible paper, such as printer paper or newsprint • Glitter yarn or string • Glitter adhesive button • Quick-setting gel glue

WHAT YOU DO
1. Embellish a package with strips of glitter tape. For tassels, adhere the glitter tapes to a 12-inch-long piece of the flexible paper. Cut evenly spaced strips in the paper, stopping 1 inch from the top. Cut the paper in half.
2. Apply a line of glue, along with a piece of glitter yarn or string, along the top of one of the cut papers. Roll the paper so it forms a tassel; hold with your finger for a few minutes so the glue sets. Repeat for the second tassel. Attach the tassels to a wrapped package by adhering the strings with a glitter of adhesive button, applying glue for extra hold.

Tree Topping

Instead of putting packages under the tree, put a tree on a package. Coffee stir sticks wrapped in paper tapes form the simple tree. Attach sequin "ornaments" for added sparkle, or leave the center blank to write the gift recipient's name.

WHAT YOU NEED
3 or 4 flat coffee stir sticks • Paper tape such as Washi tape • Quick-setting gel glue • Sequins in various sizes and shapes • Small star

WHAT YOU DO
Lay out 3 stir sticks to form a triangular tree; if needed, trim to make a shape that fits the package. Use a trimmed scrap for the trunk. Wrap the stir sticks with paper tape. Glue the edges of the tape-wrapped stir sticks to the wrapped package, forming the tree. Glue on sequin "ornaments" and a star topper.

Earthy Allure

Brown paper packages wrapped up with bakers' twine take on a stylish look topped with pinecones and a glittered floral pick. A manila tag stamped with a reindeer plays into the woodlands scheme.

WHAT YOU NEED
Bakers' twine • Glittered floral pick • 3 small pinecones • Quick-setting gel glue • Rubber stamp and stamp pad • Manila tag • Double-stick tape

WHAT YOU DO
Tie twine around a package, crossing it so it forms an X on each side. Tuck sprigs from a glittered floral pick under the twine. Glue pinecones on top. Stamp the tag and slip it under the pinecones, taping if needed.

Poinsettia Topper

A Christmas classic poinsettia moves onto gifts with this paper pretty—so much more interesting than a bow!

WHAT YOU NEED
Cardstock • Six white basket-style coffee filters • Paintbrush • Watercolor paint: pearlescent red and coral • Quick-setting gel glue • Mini pom-poms • Ribbon • Tape

WHAT YOU DO
1. Trace the poinsettia leaf templates, below, onto cardstock and cut out for templates. Stack the coffee filters, then flatten them with a warm iron. Place the templates on the flattened stack of coffee filters and lightly trace around them with a pencil; cut out.
2. Prepare a mixture of equal parts red and coral paints. Paint the poinsettia leaves; let dry. Lightly fold each leaf lengthwise. Glue the side of a leaf together at the bottom. (This will form a pointed bottom and give the petal dimension.) Repeat for remaining leaves.
3. Arrange the large leaves, pearly side up, on a circle of cardstock; glue in place. Glue the smaller leaves on top, matte side up. When the glue is dry, push down in the center to flatten the interior of the poinsettia and give it a cupped appearance. Glue mini pom-poms in the center. Tape the assembled poinsettia over a wide band of ribbon on a wrapped package.

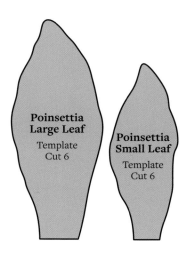

Poinsettia Large Leaf
Template
Cut 6

Poinsettia Small Leaf
Template
Cut 6

Burlap and Lace

Burlap and Lace

Textured burlap and pretty lace are layered with a quick tie of jute for a charmingly rustic gift wrap.

WHAT YOU NEED
Brown paper wrapped package • Cream and brown burlap fabric • Small strip of cream lace • Double-stick tape • Jute

WHAT YOU DO
Cut the burlap to fit around the package. Fringe the edges of the burlap. Secure with double-stick tape in the back. Use double-stick tape to attach the lace to the burlap. Tie the jute around the box.

Blooming Bow

Three fluffy hellebore-inspired flowers on the package are a delightful departure from a standard bow. Two colors of pearlescent paint give the paper petals their shimmer.

WHAT YOU NEED
Cardstock • Basket-style coffee filters • Paintbrush • Watercolor paint in pearlescent green and champagne • Floral pip • 18-gauge florist's wire • Florist's tape • Double-stick tape

WHAT YOU DO
1. Trace the template, below, onto cardstock and cut out for a template. Stack the coffee filters then flatten them with a warm iron. Place the template on the coffee filters and lightly trace around with a pencil; cut out. Brush watercolor paints on the coffee filter petals; let dry. (Flowers shown have narrow tips painted green and the top part champagne.)
2. Tape the floral pip to the wire. Arrange 3 petals around the pip, spacing them equally and adhering with florist's tape. Tape remaining petals to the wire, layering on top of the other petals. Gently bend the petals to create the desired look. Tuck the stem beneath ribbon on a wrapped package or tape in place.

Blooming Bow

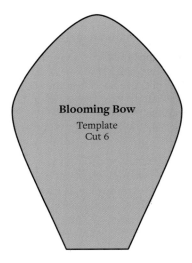

Blooming Bow
Template
Cut 6

Index

Stitch Diagrams

Backstitch

Straight Stitch

Chain Stitch

Whip Stitch

French Knot

Buttonhole Stitch

Running Stitch

Fern Stitch

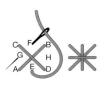
Star Stitch

Stem Stitch

Sources

Jingle Poinsettia Ornaments and Wreath, pages 14-17
Fresh-Picked Felt Wreath, pages 56-57
www.nationalnonwovens.com

Mason Jar Jewelry, pages 146-147
Polished pieces of glass drilled and ready to make or
    complete kits available upon request
Also available, Mason jar wind-chime kit
Jeff Plath and Diane Ritter
Taylors Falls Bead Store
364 Bench Street
Taylors Falls, MN 55084
Email: nnlbeads@gmail.com
www.tfbeadstore.com

Paint
www.deltacreative.com
www.plaidonline.com

Paper/Scrapbooking Supplies
www. hobbylobby.com
www. michaels.com

Paper tape/ribbon
www.cutetape.com

Pierced Tin Candles, page 138
www. homedepot.com

Sparkling Glitter Trims, page 86
Teardrop ornaments
www.hobbylobby.com

Craft Designers

Judy Bailey • Jan Carlson • Sonja Carmon •
Donna Chesnut • Carol Field Dahlstrom •
Michelle Edwards • Pam Koelling • Jeff Plath •
Susan Parsons • Suzonne Stirling • Diane Ritter •
Diane Sudhoff • Carol Schalla • Jan Temeyer